Athens Memories
THE WPA
FEDERAL WRITERS' PROJECT
INTERVIEWS

Athens Memories

THE WPA
FEDERAL WRITERS' PROJECT
INTERVIEWS

Edited by Al Hester

AN ATHENS–CLARKE COUNTY BICENTENNIAL

PUBLICATION

The Green Berry Press

ATHENS, GEORGIA

© 2001 by Albert Lee Hester

Athens, Georgia U.S.A.

Library of Congress Control Number: 2001094519

ISBN 0-9673027-7-3 (Paper)

Edited by Al Hester (Albert Lee Hester)

Production by Betty McDaniel

Printed and bound by McNaughton & Gunn

The Green Berry Press

191 E. Broad Street

Suite 322

Athens, GA 30601

Phone/FAX: 706-549-8680

First Printing September, 2001

*This book is dedicated to the memory
of the hard-working writers and editors
of the Federal Writers' Project who created
the Athens Life Histories during the Great Depression,
and to those Athens residents, poor or rich, black or white,
who told them their stories of hard times and happy times.*

Contents

ᘒ᯽ᛞ᯽ᘒ

viii CONTENTS

List of Illustrations

Acknowledgments

All Americans are indebted to the Library of Congress for its superlative efforts in making the American Life Histories available to the public. The Athens interviews and many others have been digitized and are now available at the Library's home page on the World Wide Web. These Federal Writers' Project manuscripts are just a few of the many interesting historical and cultural documents now easily available for the first time. Without this ready access to the American Life Histories, this book would have been much harder to do.

I would also like to express my appreciation for the strong support of the Athens-Clarke County Heritage Foundation and its Athens-Clarke Bicentennial Committee, co-chaired by Diane Adams and Sandi Turner. Athenians have been enriched by the group's sponsorship of many Bicentennial events and projects which tell us more about ourselves.

Also special thanks goes to Ben Epps, Jr. for sharing his knowledge about his father and for the use of photographs. I also thank Robert Young, grandson of Mary Willingham, for his help and photographs of his grandmother. The staff of Ebenezer West Baptist Church also were most helpful in gathering information about Mrs. Willingham, a longtime member of that church.

I am most grateful to Mrs. Frances Crane Epps Brame for letting me use several fine family photographs of George Shaw

Crane. And I also thank the University of Georgia's Sports Communication staff for locating a photo of the 1893 football team, which included George Shaw Crane.

I also wish to thank Karen Kelloes, archivist for Clarke County, who went beyond the call of duty, helping me find old tax records involving the Rev. Alonzo Powers. Dr. James Washington, minister at New Grove Baptist Church, was also most helpful in discussing Harriet Powers and Alonzo Powers and their association with the church.

Nelson Morgan and the rest of the staff were also most diligent and helpful in furnishing postcards from the Dean Tate Postcard Collection in the Hargrett Rare Books and Manuscripts Collections. All of us who have done books of an historical nature about Athens owe them a vote of thanks.

Jeff Weinberg most generously made the postcard of the Samaritan Building available. Nancy Lukasiewicz, curator of the Lyndon House Art Center, and Larry Forte, gallery assistant at Lyndon House, went the second mile in making the Samaritan postcard available, even though it was being used in their splendid exhibit on "Vanishing Athens."

Also, I am most grateful to Sandy Hudson of the University of Georgia Press and to Judy Long of Hill Street Press for helpful tips about book publishing.

Don Nelson of the *Athens Banner-Herald* was supportive and used an extract of one of the book's interviews for a tabloid Bicentennial publication. John English was enthusiastic about the book and helped in the publication of the extract from the Rev. Alonzo Powers interview which Don Nelson used. The book would not have been possible without the skills of Betty McDaniel of the University of Georgia Press, who as a free-lancer did the design and production for this book.

And finally, I want to thank my wife, Conoly, for her many days of hard work in reading proof, her suggestions, and for her extensive knowledge of the history of Athens.

Al Hester
Athens, Georgia
August, 2001

December 13, 1938
Mariah Jackson (Negro)
181 Lyndon Row
Athens, Georgia
(midwife)

Grace McCune, writer

CINDY WRIGHT

A search for Cindy's abode led up and down Georgia's
steep, red hills that in this particular section had been converted into slick red mire by a downpour of rain. My frequent
inquiry "Can you direct me to Cindy Wright's house?" invariably
received the response, "It's just 'round de corner to your
right." But they failed to tell me how many corners were to
be turned before I would finally arrive at the four-room house
occupied by the old granny woman. Except for need of a coat
of paint the dingy little structure seemed to be in good condition. The small yard space that led from the street to the
narrow porch was clean swept. At one side was a large grassy
plot where a few late chrysanthemums were bravely trying to
hold up their heads.

Two doors confronted me as I entered the porch and my
knock on the first one was answered by a tall young Negro who
said "Cindy, she lives next door." As I extended my hand to
rap on the adjoining door it was opened by a tiny boy, black
and shiny, attired in clean blue overalls and a red sweater.
"I heared you ax for Cindy; she's right here if you wants to
see 'er." A small mulatto woman came to the door. "I'se
Cindy," she said. "Won't you come in and set down?"

This is a page of the typescript submitted from Athens for the
American Life Histories collected by the Works Progress
Administration's Federal Writers' Program.

Introduction

The Great Depression put millions of Americans out of work, leaving many bewildered and bereft of resources they had taken for granted. Even before the 1929 stock market crash, American business was declining. By the end of 1929, stock market losses were forty billion dollars.

Within the next few years five thousand banks closed and more than 32,000 businesses went bankrupt. In 1931, twelve million persons were out of work.

From 1931 until 1940, joblessness was in the double digits and reached a peak of about 25 per cent in 1933. It is difficult for us today to realize the impact upon the country. Farmers fought off mortgage foreclosures with pitchforks, and the call came for radical action to help Americans. Brought up with a desire for self-support, most citizens waged a good battle but found they were nearly helpless against factory closings, layoffs and farm poverty.

States tried to mobilize their relief efforts, but the Depression was too big to be handled by states alone. With the election of Franklin D. Roosevelt, the United States began a complex attempt to help the country survive the economic catastrophe.

Perhaps the best known federal program to keep people off charity was the Works Progress Administration, also sometimes known as the Works Projects Administration. Americans in general didn't favor a dole and believed that citizens should do useful work for money received to help them when they couldn't get a job, and the WPA tried to carry out this ideal.

During 1935 nearly two million Americans were put to work on manual labor WPA projects, according to Grace Adams, writing in *Harpers Magazine* of October, 1938. She noted that the help programs were not allowed to compete with private industry in what it did.

"In every community throughout the nation there were roads that needed leveling, parks that needed sprucing up, public buildings that needed improvements," she said.

Adams estimates that there were about 700,000 men and women who also got help from the WPA on "white-collar projects" between 1935 and 1938. It seemed to make sense that people who had skills should get work assignments in keeping with their abilities.

One "white-collar" project of the WPA was the Federal Writers' Project. It was approved in June, 1935, with Henry Alsberg as its director. Not only were out-of-work writers helped, but just about anyone reasonably literate might be hired. Adams quotes an estimate by Ralph M. Easly of the National Civic Federation that only 21 per cent of Federal Writers' Project employees in New York City had ever written anything professionally.

The back-bone of the Federal Writers' Project was *The American Guide* series producing well-received guidebooks about each state's touristic, cultural and historic features. Many of these have been reprinted as the most thorough, wide-ranging guides ever produced about the various states.

Katherine Kellock wrote about "The WPA Writers: Portraitists of the U. S." in an article in *The American Scholar* (No. 9, 1940). She noted that the FWP between 1935 and 1940 had produced about one hundred books and 500 shorter publications.

At its peak in March, 1936, the Writers' Project employed 7,535 persons. It continued actively until 1939, but then was deemphasized with the various states taking over much of its management. World War II effectively killed the program. It had always been a controversial idea, and some politicians and officials questioned its usefulness, feeling it was open to political infiltration by left-wing writers and organizers.

Information from the WPA indicates that pay for the writers, editors, clerks, photographers and other FWP staff members ranged from about fifty dollars a month up to a little more than one hundred dollars a month in places like New York City. Staffers worked from as little as three hours per day up to nearly a full eight-hour day. It was a subsistence wage, and no one received any overtime.

Most of the workers in the South were paid the lowest amounts. In an article, "WPA Accounting" in its Feb. 15, 1943 issue, *Time Magazine* wrote that the writers' program had spent $29,189,370 during its existence. Its output filled seven, twelve-foot-high shelves in the Department of the Interior.

This book deals with one of the lesser-known parts of the writers' program, the creation and compilation of some 2,900 "Life Histories" carried out as part of the project to collect and preserve folklore and prepare social and ethnic studies.

The "Life Histories" were to be interviews with Americans of all walks of life and all races to give a broad view of both urban and rural life. In another related project, approximately 2,000 slave narratives were also collected to preserve the recollections of an estimated two per cent of the country's former slaves.

Each state had a writers' project. There was a state director, and a supervisor for each WPA region of the state. In Georgia there were nine regions. Clarke County was in Region 6. After the interviews were collected and edited in Athens, they usually went to the regional supervisor in Region 7 in Augusta for final approval. From there most of the interviews made their way to Washington.

The manuscripts of these collected Life Histories are a portion of the Library of Congress' larger Federal Writers' series and of the WPA collection. A list of all the Athens interviews is in Appendix III. The Life Histories have now been digitized by the Library of Congress, along with the slave narratives. Some are fragmented and so riddled with insertions and deletions it is very difficult to piece them together. Others, however, are fairly coherent. They are available on the Library of Congress Worldwide Web Site.

I have selected and edited nearly half of the interviews compiled in Athens as reflecting a diversity of interviewees from all walks of life. In some cases, interviews have been edited to remove redundant or less interesting material. Dialect has been modified to make the interviews more readable. Enough has been maintained to give a "feel" for the way the interviewees talked. Limitations on the size of the book and also readability considerations entered into the decisions to make some interviews more concise, to select certain interviews and to decrease the amount of dialect.

The Athens interviews made up more than half of all those done in Georgia. I must say that the quality of the Athens interviews is generally higher than most of the interviews carried out in other localities. I have also found this to be true in the slave narratives from Georgia—the Athens accounts are generally superior. The quality of the Athens interviews may be due to the interviewing skills, editing or supervision of the project. Another possibility is that the overall education level in Athens was higher because of the presence of the state's major university.

While it grates upon our ears, the "N-Word" has been retained when it was used by blacks being interviewed. It was a common mode of expression for the time. The interviews contained no examples of whites using the term. There are other examples of what today seem racist or inappropriate expressions in the interviews. These have been kept because it lets us know something about the culture and society of the 1930s.

Life History interviewers were instructed to disguise real names of their interview subjects. They did, however, use the real names in information given along with their manuscripts. I have used the real names of persons and of businesses, since there is no need for fictitious names so long after the interviews were gathered. Interviewers were inconsistent in disguising the names of family members mentioned but not interviewed. Some are real names and others are made up. In a few cases, street names were changed.

Historians who wish to view the entire collection as filed in Washington in the 1930s may consult the manuscripts in the Library of Congress.

Readers should realize that while interviewers attempted to be as accurate as possible, they did not have tape recorders, nor did they use existing phonograph recording technologies, which were cumbersome and rarely available.

The Athens interviewers were not professional writers, and the quality of interviews produced is uneven. They were governed in the structure of the interviews by directions given to them by the Federal Writers' Project. This often produced a "set-piece" effect that had the advantage of standardizing information somewhat from the interviewees, but at the sacrifice of spontaneity on the part of the interviewer.

How accurate are the interviews? I believe that generally they succeed in giving us a vignette of the lives of the people interviewed and draw us into the details of their daily life during the Depression and prior to that. In some instances I have been able to verify the accuracy of the interviews. Because of its special interest, I have spent much time in verifying information in the interview given by the Rev. Alonzo C. Powers. He is especially noteworthy because he was a son of Harriet Powers, who has become famous for the originality and quality of two of the quilts she produced late in the nineteenth century. Appendix I goes into detail about the verification of what her son said, because it throws light upon who Harriet Powers' master and mistress were in slave days and where she was born.

The Omie Williams Epps interview also received high marks for taking us into the life of the widow of Ben Epps, who built Georgia's first successful airplane in 1907. Ben Epps, Jr., her eldest son, verified a number of the points in the interview when I told him some of the details in it.

The Mary Willingham interview details also received confirmation from her grandson, with whom I discussed them. He said incidents mentioned were true-to-life.

While an imperfect representation of the life histories of the persons interviewed, the written interviews succeed admirably in giving us the feel of Athens, from the late 1800s to the 1930s.

I have tried to find out as much as possible about the interviewees, and where possible have in an introductory note given some of their vital statistics. Where possible in the short time available to publish this book during the Athens-Clarke Bicentennial I have tried to obtain photographs of interviewees, their families, or of the still-existing houses where they lived.

It is evident that no scientific, randomized sample of Athens residents was made to gather the interviews. There is evidence that sometimes the interviewers knew those interviewed, or had received suggestions to interview them. In one case the writer basically produces her own Life History. In another Life History, the interviewer recounts the WPA experience of a WPA staff member in Athens. These were included because they contain information about a writer in the program and because they throw light on how the WPA worked in Athens.

The sessions are from a mix of black and white interviewees and across a broad economic spectrum. All the interviewers and editors in Athens were white, as was generally the case throughout Georgia. There were, however, two black writers in the state project, but neither wrote about Athens residents. The interviews give us considerable insight into relations between the races, and a frequently patronizing attitude is discernible upon the part of the interviewers in some cases.

All the writers and editors in the interviews used about Athens residents were women, and this probably had the effect of fewer men being interviewed. It is quite noticeable, however, that the women interviewers seemed to have no fear of going to houses throughout the town, in both black and white areas, and in areas of rich and poor residents, by themselves, to obtain the interviews. They seem to have been hospitably received, and we can yearn for a time when crime was minor and community trust was very evident. Athens was a small town of about 22,000 persons during the Depression, and the small-town "feel" is quite evident.

Interviews in Athens were conducted by Leola T. Bradley, Ina B. Hawkes, Sadie B. Hornsby, and Grace McCune. Editors of the interviews in Athens included Sarah H. Hall, Maggie B. Freeman and John N. Booth, an area supervisor in Augusta for the Georgia Writers' Project. Booth also did secondary editing on most of the Athens interviews. I don't know whether they were edited again at the state or national level, but suspect in some cases they were.

The following information is given about the writers and editors of the Athens project:

Mrs. Leola T. Bradley was born in Dublin, Laurens County, Georgia, one of seven children She was a research field worker for the Georgia Writers' Project and in the 1938 *Athens City Directory* was shown living at 347 Hill St. The directory also lists her as the widow of L. D. Bradley, who is further identified in the cover information for her manuscript as Louie D. Bradley.

She wrote about herself for the Life Histories, indicating she lived at 424 S. Lumpkin St. on Sept. 27, 1939, at the time she wrote the article. She was identified in the manuscript edited by Mrs. Maggie B. Freeman as being an "ex-teacher and a WPA worker." Mrs. Bradley died at the age of 77 on July 2, 1967, in Fulton County, Georgia.

Although not strictly an oral Life History, the self-interview is included for the information given about WPA activities and the background of one of the WPA workers in Athens.

Mrs. Maggie Freeman was another of the Writers' Project editors working in Athens. No other information is available at this time.

Sarah Hall was also one of the Writer's Project editors working in Athens. No other information is available.

Mrs. Ina B. Hawkes was a Writers' Project writer and interviewer, working in the Athens office. She was listed as a seamstress for the WPA in the 1938 *Athens City Directory*, and she lived at 373 W. Hancock Ave. A Mrs. Ina Belle Hawkes of Jonesboro, Georgia, died June 25, 1972, in Jonesboro, according to her obituary in the *Atlanta Constitution*. The list of survivors shows two sisters living in Athens. It is probable this is the Athens writer for the WPA.

Mrs. Sadie B. Hornsby was a writer and interviewer for the Athens WPA. Death indexes have been checked with no positive result, as none of the Sadie Hornsbys listed died in Clarke County.

Mrs. Grace McCune is listed in the 1938 *Athens City Directory* as living at 675 Cobb St. Her job is given as "research worker U.S. Federal Writers Project." No records have been located about the date of her death.

Al Hester, Ph.D.
Athens, Georgia
August, 2001

Athens Memories

THE WPA
FEDERAL WRITERS' PROJECT
INTERVIEWS

Reminiscence of a Negro Preacher

Editor's Note: The Rev. Alonzo C. Powers was interviewed by Mrs. Ina B. Hawkes on Oct. 31, 1939. The interview was edited by Mrs. Maggie B. Freeman of the Athens Georgia Writers' Project office. At the time of the interview, the Rev. Mr. Powers, a Baptist minister, was living on Rural Route #1 on the Danielsville Road. He is shown as living at 161 Brays Alley in Athens in the 1938, 1940 and 1942 city directories. Brays Alley was a short street near the Danielsville Road in North Athens. He is not mentioned in later directories.

Alonzo Powers was a son of Mrs. Harriet Powers, a former slave who has become internationally known for her outstanding "Bible quilts," one of which is in the Smithsonian National Museum of American History and one in the Boston Museum of Fine Arts.

While the Rev. Mr. Powers gives 1859 as his birthdate, the Clarke County 1920 federal census says he was born about 1860, as did the 1870 and 1880 Clarke County federal censuses. (He and the rest of the Powers family were mistakenly listed as "Powell" instead of Powers in the 1880 census.) In the 1900 census, however, he is listed as being born in May, 1865. In the 1910 census, he is listed as being born about 1865.

Because of the interest in Harriet Powers and her family, I have treated the story of the Rev. Mr. Powers in more detail in Appendix I, with some comments about the accuracy of his recollections, based upon contemporary records.

• • •

In talking to the owner of a tourist camp one day, I asked the whereabouts of a Negro by the name of Alonzo Powers. The owner replied, "Yes, he lives the third house down that lane. You know he is a preacher?"

I answered that I didn't and then added that I would be glad to have the chance to talk to a colored preacher. I went down the white, sandy lane and found a two-room house. It had no front yard at all, no grass or trees for shade and no porch.

I knocked on the door and a man answered.

"Who do you want to see?" he asked. I told him I wanted to see Alonzo Powers. In a short time I heard a door shut, and I looked around and saw an old man walking around the house.

"Yes, ma'am, this is Alonzo," he volunteered.

"Good morning! Good morning Uncle!" I said. "Do you have a little time to spare this morning?"

"Yes, ma'am," he said, with a broad smile.

It was a cool day, although the sun was shining very bright. I asked him to sit in the sun so we could talk better.

I found that Uncle Alonzo had a very good education for a Negro of his type and that his English was fairly good.

He seemed to know what I came for because he said: "Well, I was born in Madison County, six miles from Danielsville, about eighty years ago in 1859. I was a slave, Miss, but a happy one.

"My young Mistess and Marster's names were Nancy and John Lester. My father's Marster's name was Jimmie Nunn. He lived on the Danielsville Road. My father would have to get a pass from Mr. Jimmie to come to see my mother. You see, they were on different plantations. He got to come to see my mother twice a week. If he slipped out without the pass the 'patterollers' got after him and if he out-run them and got back to his Marster he was safe, but if he didn't, he got a whipping. Twenty-five licks was what he would get.

"As far back as I can remember is when us little niggers was just big enough to run around. Mistess would be so good to us. She would always pay us in some way to help her.

"She would say, 'Bring me some water; git me some on the north side of the spring so it will be cool', or 'Pick up some bark for me and I will make some candy for my little niggers.'

"Lawd, Miss, you ought to have seen us little niggers scramble after that water and pick up those chips. My Mistess would not let anyone whip us, not even my mother or father. Sometimes her daughter, Miss Sallie, would get mad with us for a trifle and start to whip us. You ought to have heard us yell, 'Old Mistess, Old Mistess!'

"Out she would come. Her curse word was, 'Drat your infernal soul.' 'You just want to beat my little niggers to death,' she would say. Then Miss Sallie would leave a-running.

"Oh, we were the happiest little souls in the world. Old Miss would never consult a doctor. She was as good as any of them. When we got sick, we didn't say 'stomach.' We would holler, 'Old Mistess,' and she would come a-running and ask, 'What is the matter with my little niggers now?'

"'My belly hurts,' I'd say. She always kept some medicine made of chinaberry roots. 'Now take this, and Mistess will give you some candy.'

"My grandma was the cook. She would throw a ten-foot pole [on the fire] and let it burn to ashes and then make pones of bread. She would then put them in the ashes, and when they cooked a while she took the shovel and throw ashes over them. When they were done, she taken 'em out and washed them and greased them. Yes ma'am, they was good.

"We would go to the bottoms and find mussel shells, That is where we got our spoons that we ate with. We had plenty to eat; you see, Mistess and young Marster wanted their niggers to grow up healthy like our father. He was a big, healthy nigger. They would say, 'It ain't no trouble for a big, healthy nigger to get married.'

"I remember one time they was sending us out to hoe cotton.

I decided I didn't want to go, so I pitched a big fit. Instead of hoeing the cotton, I laid down and started grabbing it with my teeth. Marster came out and sent me to the house.

"He said I never would amount to nothing. He didn't let me go to the field no more that year. He thought I was sick.

"There was plenty of potatoes, corn, wheat and everything else that is raised on a farm, but Marster would never raise over one bale of cotton. We had ox carts in those days. I can remember when it taken two weeks to go to Augusta and back with that bale of cotton. Shoes were brought back for us all. Mistess got a dress and the rest was brought back in money.

"I remember when we didn't have no gins; us little niggers would pick out the seed with our hands. My mother would card it; my grandma would spin it. She put it on brooshes and made a bank. Every time it filled it would click. Then she started another one.

"Young Mistess was the weaver and she made all our clothes. That reminds me, Miss, we just wore one garment, a long dress. The only way I could tell the difference in my sister's clothes and mine was mine had a little yoke on it.

"We used to all go to the same church, colored and white. We would sit on one side. I would always go with my grandma. She would put her shoes in her pockets and when we got in a mile of the church she put her shoes on. When we left, she would pull them off and go on home bare-footed.

"The preacher made my Uncle Harry a deacon, and when they served bread and wine, Uncle Harry would come down the aisle and pass it around. You know, Miss, they had to break the ice to baptize. Uncle Harry's churches was not up to date like they are now.

"Us niggers had to have a pass anywhere we went, church and all. They never kept you from going anywhere, but you had to

This is the only known photo of Harriet
Powers, the mother of the Rev. Alonzo
Powers. It was probably taken in the
late nineteenth century.
Photo credit: New Grove Baptist Church

have that pass and it read 'pass' and 're-pass.' There would be 25 white men who were 'patterollers,' as I have told you before, and they would watch and could tell when one of the Negroes didn't have a pass; his feet just would not stay on the ground, 'cause he was so nervous.

"When we had big dances, the 'patterollers' would be in the middle; us slaves would be on each end, and if the 'patterollers' made a start to arrest one of the Negroes for disobedience, we would always have a fire and one of us would dip up a shovel of hot coals and throw it at them. By the time they got through dodging the hot coals, we would be gone home to our white folks.

"Some of our happy days was when we hauled up the corn and we could swing on the wagons. They was sho' happy days. You know, Miss, in slavery time if any of the slaves was disobedient, their owner's would hold them 'til the speculators came around. Then they was sold.

"If the women had children, it made no difference—they had to leave them. Or if the man had a wife, he had to go just the same.

"I remember when the Yankees came through, one big Yankee come up to my pa and said, 'I will give you my horse and blanket if you will show me all the old rich bugs.'

"Pa said, 'Wait—let me get my shoes.'

"Instead of putting on his shoes, he run through the house and yelled, 'Everybody turn loose the horses.' All the Yankees horses were old, broke-down horses and they would take ours.

"If a man wore a vest, the Yankees thought he had a watch. One big Yankee walked up to Uncle Harry and said, 'Take off that vest.' Another one said, 'Let the damn fool alone. Can't you see he has no watch.'

"All the time Uncle Harry had it hid under the wood pile. Just as soon as Uncle Harry got a chance, he threw his vest in the swamp.

Detail from the Harriet Powers "Bible Quilt." This shows the Holy
Spirit descending as a dove at the baptism of Jesus.
Photo credit: New Grove Baptist Church

"One Yankee walked up to Mistess and said, 'How come you got such a big bosom—give me all that money.'

"Mistess said, 'I haven't got any money.'

"The Yankee took his knife and cut Mistess' dress open, and gold and silver went everywhere. It was awful.

"Mr. Franklin was my Marster's older brother. The Yankees got him and hung him up by his toes. He would not tell where his money was. Then they hung him up by his neck; he could hardly whisper. Still he would not tell them where his money was.

"The Yankee yelled at one of his men to bring him the auger. He got poor old Mr. Franklin down and started boring in his head. Mr. Franklin said, 'Please don't kill me. I will tell, it is under a pile of rocks in the garden, in an old trunk.'

"They got all of poor old Mr. Franklin's money.

"Yes ma'am, Miss, we stuck to our Marster and Mistess. When they trusted their niggers, they would give them all their valuables to keep or hide for them.

"I can see one of the niggers on the place now. Marster gave him his watch to keep for him. He put it in his vest pocket. The chain stretched across his stomach. He walked out where the other niggers was, pretending they was Yankees. He rared back and put his fingers on his vest and said, 'Now take it away from me like you would old Marster.'

"He was so proud to get to wear his Marster's watch.

"The Yankees made my mother cook fifteen bushels of peas and three middlins of meat. They didn't wait for them to get done. The peas just got hot and swelled. They taken them and left with all the good horses they could catch of ours and all the money they could find.

"If our Marster and Mistess saw a big, healthy nigger, it won't no trouble to get him married, for they would urge it on.

"Yes ma'am, I know you have heard about when people got

married—a saying of 'jump the broom.' I will tell you about that. It didn't make no difference, white or colored, if there was a wedding you could hear it all around.

"'Are you going to the broom jumping tonight?' folks would ask. Everybody would go. You see, Miss, we had straw brooms back in those days. One was fixed about the size around my arm, and five feet long. It was laid down on the floor. Everybody would gather around. The man and woman that was going to marry would stand by the broom. The preacher would say to the man, 'Do you take this woman to be your wife?' He says, 'Yes.'

"'Well, jump the broom.' After he jumped, the preacher would say the same to the woman. When she jumped, the preacher said, 'I pronounce you man and wife.' That's how all marriage ceremonies were then.

"My young Marster went to war to substitute for Mr. Franklin. Miss, it seems as if I can see him now. He called me 'Ding.' He said, 'Here, Ding, take this big, red apple, and if you don't ever see Marster again, remember me by it.'

"I never did see him no more. He got killed fighting. Mistess got forty dollars, but it was no good, because we lost young Marster.

"They called old John in to pray for Marster. John was a big nigger. His prayer was, 'God bless young Marster in the war, and give them their victory, and bless old Marster and Mistess at home.'

"Going home, his wife Mary said, 'John, how in the devil do you ever expect to be set free and you praying like that?'

"Old John looked at Mary and said, 'God knows what I mean.'"

Uncle Alonzo sat very quietly for a moment as if he were seeing everything over again. He took a long breath and smiled.

"Lord, Miss, them was some days."

"How old were you, Uncle Alonzo, at the time of the surrender?" I asked.

"That's where I began another life, Miss. I was ten years old. My father sent me to several different schools. We stayed on at the old plantation though. My father and mother could stay together now, and they worked and we had plenty. Lots of the old niggers were left without anything.

"My father would raise a bunch of hogs and put them in the cellar and sell them at a very high price. I can remember him selling wheat at sixty dollars a bushel. He made a pair of rawhide shoes one time and sold them for one hundred dollars to Mr. Ledbetter.

"This is something else I want to tell you: My father cut down maple trees and let them dry. Then he made little pegs and used them for nails to make his shoes. He was a very smart man.

"I kept going to school walking fourteen miles every day, but I liked it, and I finally got my license and taught for several years.

"I met a girl then and fell in love with her. Mr. Bob Yerby married Julia Jackson and me. We lived at New Grove, Georgia.

"I decided that I wanted to give my work and soul to God. So I worked in the field by myself and picked three hundred pounds of cotton every day. I could chop three acres a day and made twelve bales of cotton and all the food I needed for my mule and cows.

"I taken this and went to see about my studies for a preacher. I studied theology under Dr. Lyons and Dr. Clark. I can't remember when I joined the church, but it was over fifty years ago. I have lived in Clarke County all my life except ten years and have been a pastor for over twenty churches: in Atlanta, and in Greene, Oglethorpe, Madison, Oconee, Jackson, Banks, and Gwinnett counties. I have baptized over three thousand people. God help me how many knots have I tied.

"I lived on at New Grove. Julia and me had fourteen children—all good healthy children. I stayed on 'til all the children died but five, and when Julia died, I left New Grove. The children was grown anyway. I come to Athens, but I was pastor at Comer, Georgia. Willie, Sue, and Ophelia went to Richmond, Virginia. My oldest son died in Johnstown, Pa., during the World War."

"Uncle Alonzo, how about your other son. Where is he?" I asked.

"He lives here with me. He is a preacher, too. His church is at Allenville. Even though he is my son, Miss, I don't want to brag, but he is a very intelligent boy. As I have said, I am still pastor at Comer. I failed in health some, and I asked them to get another preacher, but they never have.

"I still go and preach when I can. I preached yesterday, and my text was the Eighth Psalm—a Psalm of David.

"Yes ma'am, Miss, I have been a great man. When I walk in a church now, men draw up in knots. God breathed life into the nostrils of man so we could do great things for Him.

"Yes ma'am, Miss, I used to go to Mr. Walter Jones' home on Milledge Avenue one time a year and preach him a sermon as long as he lived. I am going there Christmas and preach a sermon for his son, if I am living. All his kinfolks from Baltimore are coming.

"I train all the bird dogs for them. You know they like to hunt and I do, too. Young Mr. Jones takes me now to the plantation for a week to hunt and train his dogs. He always pays my board to some of the tenants out there. I have a time with them dogs.

"Sometimes Mr. Jones's friend comes out on week-ends and hunts. This friend always brings his dogs with him. He had one great big dog. One of ours was small. These two dogs got to fighting one day and ours won.

"This man said, 'How is it your little dog can always whip my big dog?' I told him it wasn't always the size that whipped.

"Not long ago I was preaching in Greene County. After the meeting was over, the boys all wanted to go hunting. They insisted that I go with them. Well, I thought it would be good sport, so I went. We hunted all around and finally spotted a 'possum on a limb way out over a river. Well, it was night and you know, Miss, how scary it looks out on a river bank at night. Everybody wanted to know who was going out after the 'possum.

"The big nigger said he would go. So he gave a big jump and caught the limb."

Uncle Alonzo was holding his hands up to show me how the Negro did and laughing so he could hardly tell me.

"Well, he hung on there and saw he could not get down without falling in the water. He began to yell for some of us to come out and help him. We told him it was impossible, for we could not go out there.

"'Please come out and help me,' he cried.

"'No, we can't.'

"'Well,' he said, 'tell Nancy to meet me in heaven.' That's his wife.

"He began to pray, 'Oh Lord, please save me.' About that time the limb broke and he grabbed the one below. He kept on praying, 'Lord, have mercy.'

"The limb he was holding broke then, and into the water he went. It struck him just above the waist. He looked all around and said, 'Hell, it wasn't as deep as I thought it was.'

"It is all through life like that, Miss. I am old now, but the white folks are good to me, though. God bless you."

An Air-Minded Family

❧❀❀❀❧

Editor's Note: Mrs. Omie Williams Epps was the widow of Benjamin Thomas Epps, one of the nation's aviation pioneers. Ben Epps opened the first gasoline station in Northeast Georgia, according to Mrs. Epps, but his true passion was airplanes. He built his first plane in 1907, only four years after the Wright Brothers made their first flight. The Athens airport, Ben Epps Field, is named for him. He died in 1937 in a crash of one of his planes at the Athens airfield. He was fifty years old. His and Mrs. Epps' surviving children still maintain an active interest in aviation, and have an aviation business in Atlanta.

Mrs. Epps died June 19, 1955. She was seventy-one years old. The Epps home at 892 Hill St. still exists in good condition. Mrs. Epps was interviewed by Mrs. Sadie B. Hornsby on March 6, 1939, and said she was a saleslady at that time.

• • •

I asked the taxi driver if he knew just where Mrs. Epps lived.

"Yes ma'am," he said, at the same time stopping in front of a one-story red brick house, with the woodwork painted white. Hyacinths, forsythia and jonquils were in full bloom. These flowers bordered the spacious, green lawn and low shrubbery surrounded the house.

A lattice fence, with an opening just large enough for a car to go through, screened the back yard. There were flowers in full bloom in the back yard, just as in front, with low shrubbery close to the house and garage.

A wash pot was turned upside-down, and there was a play-house in the yard. Parts of a demolished airplane were in the garage.

I knocked on the door, and a voice called to me: "Just open the door and come in. I am too lazy to get up."

I entered the living room, and there sat Mrs. Epps, dressing a small, black-haired, blue-eyed little girl about four years old.

"Do have a chair—if I don't dress Sissie before I get up, she won't let me get her dressed. I haven't made a fire in the furnace and the house is none too warm. The maid hasn't come yet and everything is topsy-turvy," Mrs. Epps explained.

As she talked about this and that, I glanced around the room. It was evident that a member the family worked for an electric company. There were three lamps in this room—one on the ra-dio, another on a marble-top, antique table and a floor lamp by a Governor Winthrop desk.

There were several antique chairs, a modern three-piece living-room suite, a bookcase filled with books on aeronautics, two mir-rors and several pictures on the wall.

A clock and pictures of Mrs. Epps' two grown sons were on the mantel, as well as a picture of her deceased husband, Ben Epps, who was a well-known aviator. A picture of her oldest daughter was on a desk.

A rug with pink roses in block design and criss-cross curtains with blue ball trimmings completed the furnishings in this room.

Mrs. Epps finished dressing the child, turned out the light, and came over near the window where I was sitting on the red, uphol-stered divan. She picked up a sweater and began darning it.

"My boys won't wear these sweaters because there is a touch of red on them. It isn't necessary to do this mending this morning, but I thought I might as well be doing something while I am talk-ing. It is such a bad day I can't get out and sell my cosmetics.

An early picture of Mrs. Omie Epps,
widow of Ben Epps
Photo credit: Ben Epps, Jr.

Ben Epps displays his first airplane, built in his garage in downtown
Athens in 1907. Epps went on to become an aviation pioneer.
Photo credit: Hargrett Rare Book & Manuscript Library,
University of Georgia

This handsome plane was built by Ben Epps,
standing in the picture, in the 1920s.
Photo credit: Ben Epps, Jr.

"My battery is no good on my car, so I will have to wait another day. When I go out, I take the two small children with me and leave them in the car while I make my calls selling my product. I also sell Christmas cards in season.

"My children fuss with me because I get out and work, but I have worked all my life and know what it takes to live on. Too, I don't feel right to sit down and let my older children take care of me and the ones who are not large enough to work.

"So after the Negro finishes her work and dinner is over, I put the children in the car, take my cosmetic kit and try to do my bit. Some days I do real well, and some days I get so discouraged I feel like giving up, but I can't.

"But what is it you want me to tell you? I have just talked and talked and you have come for my life history. Why would anybody pick me out of all people?" Mrs. Epps asked.

"You know, a mother of ten children and nine living don't have time to think about what has happened, and I'm afraid to think what might take place, after all I have been through. I have had children, and my husband has been killed.

"I am praying I won't have to go through it again. We never know what is to happen to us in this life.

"My young days was spent in Greene County at Siloam, Georgia. I was born in Madison County, out there at Neese. People in Madison County could sell their land and buy land for half-price in Greene County in those days. So my people sold their land and bought a farm near Siloam and lived in the little village. That is the way people did then.

"I was twelve years old when I went there to live, and perhaps my happiest days as a young girl was spent in that settlement.

"It was a little odd the way I started to work. There was a man who ran a general merchandise store—his daughter, who was my best friend, helped him in his business. On the day my friend was to marry—the invitations had been issued and everything set for the wedding—she ran away and married someone else.

"A few days after that, I met the girl's father on the street, and he told me his wife wanted to see me right away. Well, I was scared green—I thought sure she blamed me for the girl running away and marrying someone else. Instead, she wanted me to work in the store in her daughter's place. I accepted the job and received six dollars a month. I worked twelve hours a day. I was crazy about my job. I worked and took music lessons, too. I remember I had an argument with my family—they wanted the money for something else, and I wanted to continue my music lessons and did it. I also bought my own clothes as well as things for the house.

"My brother got a job with the Athens Railway and Electric Company. He was here about a year when I decided to write a leading store in Athens for a job, as they were the only people I had ever heard of in business.

"My people laughed at me and said, 'Why, don't you know they won't give you a job. There are so many people in Athens, they won't even answer your letter.'

"Anyway, I wrote them, and right away I received a letter from them telling me the next time I came to town to come by to see them. I lost no time coming to Athens. On going to the store and applying for the job, they told me the one who employed the girls was out sick and for me to come back the following Monday.

"As I was leaving the store, I asked them to save the job for me—that I would be back when they told me to. When I walked out of the store, the man to whom I had been talking came to the door and said to me, 'Come back when we told you to and go to work.'

"I received the big amount of fifteen dollars a month. I worked there about three years before I married and worked off and on about two years afterward. I worked as long as I could before my first child was born. As soon as I could, I went back and worked until Junior came along, then I gave up and decided there was no need trying.

"My father and mother came to town with me to live. My father went back and forth to Greene County to superintend his farms and sawmill. Mother kept house, and looked after the children, cows, chickens, etc.

"When I came here to live, I was engaged to a man studying for the Presbyterian ministry at Clemson College in South Carolina. I have had so many things said to me that turned out to be true, it frightens me for anyone to make any predictions.

"This man to whom I was engaged didn't want me to come to Athens. He said, 'You won't be there three weeks before you will meet someone you will like better than you do me.'

"I told him that was impossible, because I was in love with him and very much interested in my music. But sure enough, I hadn't been here but a short time before I met Ben.

"One day I was leaving the store going to lunch. A boy I knew was standing out in front. He called to me and said, 'Wait a minute. I have something to tell you.'"

Mrs. Epps said her future husband, Ben, was walking by.

"'Come back here, pal, I want you to meet the new girl in the store—she hasn't been in Athens long,' the boy I knew said to Ben.

"From that time on, my friend kept asking me for a date to go automobile riding. I didn't know girls went riding at night. I told my mother, and she told me it would be no harm, if there was another couple along.

"So when my friend, Ben and another girl came to my house, I didn't know I was to be with Ben until he got there. From that time on, we had dates regular. I told him I was engaged to someone else. He told me he didn't care—he was in South Carolina and Ben was here, and he was going to beat his time, and he did.

"He was like that. He started to build airplanes and wouldn't quit.

"After we married, we lived with his mother two years. Then his father and mother gave Ben a building lot just outside the city limits. We built a nice house.

"I thought I was all set with a well on the back porch, and kerosene lamps, with a nice garden, chickens, cows, and I even had a hog or two. It wasn't long before Ben put an electric pump in the well.

"After the children got large enough to go to school, it was too expensive to send so many to school in town. So I began to beg my husband, 'Let's build in town.' He told me, 'All right, but as sure as we do, one of the children will be killed sure.'

"Still, I insisted. So after living in the country thirteen years, we built this house and moved to town. Sure enough, we had only been here three years when the child next to the baby was run over in the yard and died as the result of that injury.

"He developed pneumonia and only lived a short time.

"We have been living here ten years. My husband's real business was in the garage business. He had the first filling station in Athens.

"You know every man has a hobby—his was with airplanes. When he closed his garage for the day, instead of playing golf or working in the yard or garden, he tinkered with his planes. He begun building airplanes about two years before we married. He made a short flight in 1909; in 1910 he wrote to a land company asking them to let him attend one of their land sales and take people to ride, to draw a large crowd.

"They wrote him they would take the matter up with him, and they were sure it could be made profitable for the company as well as himself, but they never did anything about it.

"The whole family is crazy on the subject of airplanes. However, when he had a smash-up, his family blamed me for not discouraging him.

"He was doing this before we married—how could I change him?

"There was no airport here to try out his planes, so he took them out to an open field to try them out. That was when he first tried to fly them. He smashed them up, hauled them in, and started all over again.

"He just took it up as a hobby and only studied it a short time in a private school in Virginia when my second girl was a baby. Ben took up this hobby a short time before the Wright Brothers flew theirs.

"Ben was never a person to talk about himself. He always brought the newspaper clippings home for me to read. Several days ago, Dr. Reid told me that he and Mr. Hugh Rowe went out with Ben at two o'clock one morning to fly his first plane.

"Back when my oldest son was fourteen, some friends took him on a trip to Washington, D. C. Mrs J. S. Grey of Chevy Chase, Maryland, was writing a book called '*UP*' *Aviation of Yesterday and Today*. It never occurred to me to mention it to my son to visit her.

So when he got to Washington, he decided to look her up. She was very much interested in him and wrote a page-and-a-half about him in her book.

"He made his first solo flight in Atlanta at an air show when he was thirteen years old. That was the first time I had ever seen him fly, and he handled it just like his daddy. When I look at these children of thirteen it frightens me to think of the things we let him do.

"As far as we know he was the youngest person to fly a plane in this country or abroad. I remember there was a mob in Atlanta at the air show. It was about dark when I started home—one of my little boys was missing. I looked everywhere in that crowd.

Later, I learned that he had flown home with his Daddy in the plane, and slept all the way.

"Yesterday Mother Epps was spending the day with me. The planes were flying overhead. I said to her, 'My little boys are dying to get out to the airport and get in one of those planes.'

"She said, 'I don't blame them—I would, too, if I was out there.'

"Ben taught lots of boys to fly. It was ten dollars an hour. He gave one man lessons to refresh his memory on flying. I had to get up when one of my babies was two weeks old and get Ben's breakfast so he could get out to the field by six o'clock to take him up and teach him two hours before he went to his garage at eight.

"That man run his bill up to eighty dollars and never paid a cent of it. He was later killed in New York. He ran into a high tension wire while flying a passenger plane over the city.

"Oh, I do wish the weather would clear up so I could get out and sell my cosmetics. You know it's my disposition to work, and I sold them during my husband's lifetime to help out. I don't make much, but now, every penny I make goes a long ways."

Mrs. Epps' daughter, who holds a responsible position with reliable company in Athens, came in.

"Good morning," her mother said, and told her what I was doing.

"That's fine," the daughter said. "Mother, I want my lunch by twelve o'clock, and while you fix it. I will make out some reports."

She went to the desk and laid her books on it. Mrs. Epps excused herself while she went to the kitchen, saying, "Now, you don't have to go. Just stay and have lunch with us."

I declined, but she said: "Now, don't go. There's no need, and after lunch we can finish what you want to know. It won't take me but a few minutes, as I cooked quite a bit yesterday. I was expecting a house full of company. They didn't come, so I am just warming it over.

"You just make your self at home. I have the most convenient way of cooking in the world."

I followed her to the kitchen where there was an electric stove, refrigerator, percolator and several other electric appliances, a kitchen cabinet, a rug on the floor and curtains at the windows.

"While the dinner is warming, I want you to see the bed my daughter had made. A woman had the lumber left from a suite she had made and sold it to her. I think it cost twenty dollars finished."

I went into the bedroom from the kitchen.

"Was this ever a breakfast room?" I asked.

"No, this is the only say-so I had about the building of this house. I told my husband, 'How in the name of the Lord can I run through the kitchen, dining room and living room to get to the bedrooms to see about one of the children if one of them is sick?' So this door was cut."

In the room was a slender, four-post bed, a vanity dresser painted green, a few scatter rugs on the floor, and a pin-up lamp still burning over the bed. This room opens into a small narrow hall. A bathroom opens into this hall. The floor is tile with tub and other conveniences.

Another bedroom opens into this hall, which is evidently the boys' room, as clothing, shoes, books and airplanes are scattered all over the room. There were two white iron beds, a dresser, a bedside table, pin-up lamp and nice blue bedspreads on the beds.

Mrs. Epps took me into another room and said: "This is my room and the babies' room. I don't have no other place for this desk my husband used in his office. I had several students staying with me. For eight months I let them have my room and the boys'.

"I have a nice, large room in the basement and we went down there to sleep. There is a shower, too. I would like to have some boarders now, but the boys don't want them.

"If I did take in boarders, then I could give up selling my cosmetics and devote all my time at home."

There was a walnut suite in her room. "Everything is so torn up this morning. I am ashamed for you to see my house. The maid came, but she didn't stay long. She is a settled woman and has to look after her affairs on Monday when I pay her off."

"Mother," asked the girl, "is lunch ready? I have got to eat and get back on the job."

"Yes, all I have to do is to put it on the table," Mrs. Epps said.

I was writing and she went to the kitchen. In a few minutes she announced that lunch was ready.

"Now, I have set a plate for you, and there is no reason why you can't have lunch with us."

Again I declined the invitation, saying I would wait until they had finished to complete the interview. Miss Epps, the daughter, said: "Oh, come on and eat with us."

So I went to the dining room with her and had lunch. The suite in this room was much too large for the size of the room. There was a large buffet, table, chairs, an old Victrola, doll carriage and a large bookcase filled with books on aeronautics. A floor lamp was placed between the windows overlooking the street. Criss-cross curtains with blue ball trimmings were at the windows; there were a few pictures on the wall and a green rug on the floor.

Miss Epps said grace, and the lunch consisted of spinach, turnips, mashed potatoes, cornbread, biscuits, banana salad, cake, coffee, and buttermilk.

"Now, help your self," invited my hostess. "Don't be afraid to eat, for there is plenty for all. I had cube steaks and gravy yesterday for lunch, so I didn't think we needed meat today. Anyway, vegetables are much better for people."

Lunch was over, and we sat chatting. Then an airplane came zooming overhead, and everyone jumped from the table—some of us ran to the window while others ran out on the front porch. After the commotion was over, Miss Epps came back into the room saying: "Gee, it was flying low."

"Did you ever fly a plane?" I asked.

"I never soloed, but I did take lessons from my father when I was about fourteen or fifteen."

"Why didn't you continue your lessons?" I asked.

"Well, the Depression came on and Father couldn't afford to take his planes up unless he was getting paid for it, so I had to discontinue them," Miss Epps explained.

Putting on her hat and coat, she was gone.

Mrs. Epps came in and began: "These children have pulled out every book their daddy had on airplanes. At night I have to pick my way to bed over model airplanes, and I find books all over the bed and even under their pillows, where they have fallen to sleep with them.

"Ben felt like he was a failure, but of course he wasn't. He went to New York about twenty years ago and bought a flying boat that had been shipped back from France. I was so busy with babies, I didn't know what he was doing. He provided for his family what he thought was necessary.

"So he had saved a little money of which I knew nothing, and bought the boat with it. He advertised it for sale for $100,000. A man who was an aviator saw the ad, wrote him, saying, 'Let's get together on the boat. You have offered it too cheap, and let's rebuild it and make some money.'

"They spent three weeks putting it in shape. Then they took it to New Jersey to fly it. The man, who was an Englishman, took it up and had to make a forced landing in a small place where there were lots of trees.

"When they tried to take it up again, they didn't have room enough to get over the trees. They had a smash-up.

"That $100,000 was gone, so they brought it back to Athens

and made a land plane out of it. They made quite a bit of money out of it. That was back when people didn't mind paying fifteen dollars to take just a short ride.

"Ben had a very dignified man helping him at the airfield. One day, several people went out for a ride. In the party was a very prim woman. That was when women wore long dresses. After the helmets, safety belts and strappings were adjusted on the people in the plane, the helper noticed the woman hadn't pulled her goggles down.

"He said to her, 'Pull your goggles down.'

"She looked at him but made no attempt to pull them down. He told her several times, and after the door to the plane was closed, he tapped on the window and yelled, 'I say, lady, pull your goggles down.'

"Then she meekly pulled up her long skirt to her knees and pulled her garters down around her ankles.

"That brought a burst of laughter from everyone who saw it. That man would get out of the way at the mention of a woman's garters.

"The money my husband made on his planes he always put back in them. The money he supported his family on was made in the garage business and filling station. He had so many smash-ups it took everything he realized from them to put them back in shape again.

"Once he was going to Florida to an air show. When they got to Macon, they stopped for gas. They had hardly got out the sight of town when he had a smash-up. He always did think the people at the filling station put cheap gas in his plane.

"When he was building his hangar, there came a terrible storm. It took one of the posts out of the ground and sat it down in the middle of his plane—as if some person had done it.

"Every time he had an accident, people would say to me. 'Well, I guess Ben won't fly any more after this.'

"I would tell him what they said. His answer was, 'I never quit.'

"The most honest thing which ever happened to him was that he had a man helping him rebuild planes. On one of them he connected the control wires backwards, and when they took it up to try it out, it worked in reverse.

"That smashed it. The man got out of the plane and walked off the field without saying a word. Several years after that Ben was in Atlanta and saw him on the street. He said to my husband: 'I want you to know when I smashed up that plane I was broke. Now I am making good and I want to pay for half of the damages done.'

"My husband took the money as he was badly in need of cash at that time.

"About fifteen years ago, Ben built a light plane of his own design and sold it. Then he built another one. My son flew it all the time, and my husband was flying it when he had his last smash-up.

"Before his death, he had lost everything we had. He often said one thing he would never do was mortgage our home. But he did, and now we are doing everything we can to save it.

"He had closed his garage and gotten a job at thirty-five dollars a week. He thought with that coming in each week and what he made on his planes we could do very well. He had only drawn one pay check.

"At one time. we were worth $40,000. Now it is a struggle to keep our heads above the water.

"Just a few nights before he was killed, he couldn't sleep," Mrs. Epps said. "It was his guarding angel warning him that something was going to happen.

"No, the Wright Brothers had no effect on him. He thought everybody was responsible for their own failure or success. He never had one penny donated him toward his enterprise.

"His death has had no effect on us as to our belief in aviation.

We are as interested in it now as we were in his lifetime. I am sure if Ben had known that was his last flight, he would have been happy to know he died or was killed in what he loved best, no matter how far he had to fall.

"His death left us without a cent. He did have two insurance policies—however, he had borrowed money on both of them. One policy had a clause in it that the policy was no good in case he was killed in an airplane accident. The other one was taken out before that clause was added in policies. To be exact, I only received five hundred dollars, and eighteen dollars, which was just enough to put him away decent.

"I have two sons in college. They work in the daytime and go to Tech at night. My oldest son is taking aeronautical engineering, and the other one is taking a plain freshman course at the same college. I have two girls who have finished college—both have good jobs. One here and the other one is teaching school at Tate, Georgia.

"One of my little boys told me not so long ago: 'Mama, did you know one day I went up with Daddy to chase the clouds and got lost?'

"'No,' I told him."

"'Well, we did. We didn't have much gas and was afraid we would have a smash-up. I am sure we were over Comer, Georgia, so we turned around and came back safe. Do you know why we weren't hurt or run out of gas?'

"'No,' I said."

"'Well, it was because after Daddy told me that we were lost in the clouds and didn't have much gas, I began to pray and prayed until we landed. When we got out of the plane, I said: 'Thank you, God, for letting us get back safe.'"

"'That's fine,' I told him, 'but you children are going to drive us to the poor house, spending every cent you get on model airplanes.'

"A few days after that, the baby said to my oldest daughter. 'Did you know we are going to move?'

"'No,' she said.

"'Well we are,' he said.

"'Where?' she asked

"'To the poor house.'

"'How are we going?'

"'In an airplane.' answered the baby.

"I know what I have told you isn't interesting, but it is our life. We are all wild about aviation. But when you need some cosmetics, please get them from me. That is where my few pennies comes from now," Mrs. Epps said.

I thanked her for the story, and started to leave.

"Do come back again," she said. "There is my daughter. She went to get a check cashed so I can pay my bills."

The telephone rang, and she closed the door. The girl was getting out of the car, belonging to her company.

"Come back again."

"Thanks," I said, and left the Epps home and the air-minded family.

"Ain't No Midwife"

Editor's Note: Mrs. Mary Phillips Willingham, a retired practical nurse, was interviewed March 14 and May 29, 1939, by Mrs. Sadie B. Hornsby, and the interview was edited by Mrs. Sarah H. Hall of the Athens WPA Writers' Project, and by John N. Booth, the Augusta area supervisor of the Writers' Project. Mrs. Willingham lived to be one hundred and two years old, dying May 25, 1990, in Clarke County, where she had been a lifelong resident.

At the time of the interviews she was living at 140 Cohen St., and the modest house still stands today. She was the widow of Arthur Willingham, Sr. She was well known to many Athens residents, both black and white. At the time of her death she was living at 258 Arch St.

Some of her favorite sayings were listed in her funeral program at Ebenezer Baptist Church West. These included: "God hasn't made any mistakes," "God hasn't forgotten you," and "Heap sees—a few knows."

• • •

"You'll have to come up on the porch and set down whilst I washes if you wants to talk to me," Mary announced, when I found her in the back yard tending the fire around the boiling wash pot.

"I meant to wash outdoors in the sunshine," she continued, "but my husband and daughter got off before I had a chanst to get 'em to move my wash bench off of the porch for me."

"I'm surprised to find you at home, Mary," I told her. "I was just taking a chance when I strolled around to the back after there was no answer to my raps on your front door. Have you given up nursing in favor of taking in washing now?"

"No, ma'am, I ain't had no nursin' job in a month now. I'm just doing my own family washing, least I is this morning. I does have two small washings. I means I calls myself having two, but the folks didn't bring 'em last week, and they ain't brung 'em so far this week."

I sat down and watched her as she worked. Mary is a stout woman of medium height. Tightly braided gray hair framed her gingerbread-colored face, and she wore a nurse's soiled blue uniform, a white apron, black slippers, and gray cotton hose.

She spat into the tub of clothes, half-heartedly rubbed a garment across the washboard a time or two, stood up straight and said, "Miss, does you know where I can git a job?"

"No," I replied.

"What!" she ejaculated. "Out of all the folks you knows!"

"That's true, Mary, I surely don't know of a job you could get right now," I told her, "but the National Reemployment Service will help you to get work if you'll register in their office."

"I did try at that place. They asked me a hundred and one questions and then some: 'What did you make? What did you spend your money for? Well, why didn't you save some of it while you was makin' it?'

"They took all them questions and washed my face with 'em. I'll bet not a one of them folks that asks them questions saves none of their own wages, yet they goes right on askin' other folks questions they wouldn't want to answer for nobody else.

"I told the one that asked me them things that the reason I couldn't save none of my money was that me and my family had to eat, buy clothes, and pay rent, let alone having to help my people when they needed it. They's been a heap of colored folks gone hungry at times in these last several years, when their own folks didn't have nothin' to provide with 'em no more.

"I sure don't know what us poor Negroes is going to do," she grumbled. "When I first started to work I got more to do than I could keep up with. Now, folks goes to the hospital, but when they gits back home some of their folks comes and stays with 'em till they's up and about again. I reckon folks just has to do that way to cut expenses."

"How long have you been a nurse?"

"Let me see now, since 1924," she answered. "You know, I ain't no midwife; I'se a practical nurse. I'se helped doctors and mid-wives, and I'se maided and cooked. Lord, have mercy! I had to spend my money fast as I could git it feedin' my family, payin' house rent, and for all the things I told that man what asked so many questions at the Employment Office.

"I got my 'stificate to do practical nursin' in 1926. It took me two years to git it. It used to be anybody could wait on a woman havin' a baby; they could go ahead and cut the cord and tie it if they knowed how. Now, that's all changed. If you don't have that 'stificate they'll put you in the penitentiary for life.

I hopes to git my next 'stificate in about another year, and then I can call myself a midwife and pull down thirty-five dollars a week. Then I won't have to worry about my meat and bread no more—leastwise not long as women keeps on havin' babies. I means to save up for a rainy day when I does git to makin' what a midwife should.

"I don't know when I was born 'cause I didn't know nothin' t'all about my Ma. I recomembers seein' my Pa, all right enough. I can guess at my age, but I really don't know jes' how old I is. I tells everybody that. I 'spect I will be almost forty-nine my next birthday. I was born on a farm down here in Clarke County, and all I ever done in my younger days mostly was work in the field. I'se just been in town about sixteen years. I used to have time and money to go see my folks, but I don't no more. Like I done told you, my Ma died when I was a baby.

"My sister raised me part of the way; then some white people took me up and I lived with 'em years and years. I lived and worked in the house with them white folks till I married.

"The first real nurse I ever seed was a white woman what they called in to nurse one of the chillun that was took bad sick out in the country. One day that nurse went out in the yard to the lavatory—folks didn't have them places in the house to set on in the country. The lavatory was hid back of a grape arbor. She was passing under the arbor on her way back to the house when a bug got in her ear. She went to the kitchen, twisted a little white somepin' 'round on a match stem, got some warm water and worked with her ear a long time.

"I thought that was fine doin's. I said to myself, 'If she can do things like that, I can, too.' Right then and there I decided to be a nurse.

"Gittin' my first case come so easy that I thought nursing was going to be a regular job. My husband's sister that was nursing a white woman took sick and give me the job. I went there and liked the work and the white folks liked me. That eight dollars a week they paid me was a whole lots more'n I coulda made cooking, or maiding, or taking in washing.

"That was a good lady what I nursed. Her aunt said that shakin' disease she had was caused by her being a senarvis [stenographer?]. She had done worked her fingers so long on a typewriter that she 'most lost use of her hands and arms, and that condition spread over her whole body.

"'Oh, please rub my legs,' she would say. 'Oh, please scratch my head. If you will only rub my back; I'm so nervous.' I had to be doing somethin' for her all the time, day and night."

Mary stopped talking long enough to spit again into the tub of clothes and to rub a few strokes on the washboard. It seemed a good time for me to ask, "Why do you spit in the clothes?"

She laughed heartily and was not the least embarrassed when

Mary Willingham, right, was more than 100 years old
when this picture was taken of her and her daughter,
Hattie Thomas. Mrs. Willingham lived to be 102.
Photo credit: Robert Young

This small house at 140 Cohen St. was one
of the residences of Mary Willingham. Taken in 2001.
Photo credit: Al Hester

she replied, "They tell me if you spit on dirty clothes it'll take the spots out when nothin' else will. So every time I sees a bad dirty spot I just up and spits on it, and it 'most always comes out without no more trouble.

"This nursin' business," she continued, "brings you up against all sorts of folks and things. Why, I even lost one job I had because the sick woman told the doctor I had said her pulse was too fast.

"'Well, if she has to go around tellin' sick folks such things, we'll let her go,' he allowed.

"I ain't never told no other sick folks about theyselfs no more.

"I couldn't git my 'stificate to do practical nursin' till I observed at least one operation, and so I got my chanst when a white woman what lived in the country come to her sister's house in town to have a tumor cut out. The colored nurse what was to help the doctors and the white nurse got to pouting so I had to take a hand, and not havin' done nothin' of the sort before, I emptied out the water with the gauzes in it and they couldn't count 'em right.

"That sure learnt me a lesson; for when that patient didn't git well like they thought she oughta, they made a 'zamination and discovered that a gauze was sewed up in 'er. Cutting her open again and taking it out never amounted to nothin', so they done that out in the country in her own house, and she got well fast enough then.

"Now don't you go blamin' them doctors. Them was grand doctors, but that little old room was too dark, in spite of that big old flashlight almost long as my arm what her husband had bought when the doctors was fussing 'cause they wasn't no electric lights in that house where they done the first operation. Besides, there was so much discharge they couldn't half see, and it was my fault for pouring out the water before them pieces of gauze could be counted.

"That colored nurse that pouted and didn't do her part on that case lost out with the doctors and they don't never call on her no more.

"Another time I helped one of them doctors remove a big tumor from a colored woman that had been suffering with it thirty years. It weighed nearly forty pounds. I have worked for that doctor many times since. He is a good man and a fine doctor, but you better watch out and not make him mad."

As Mary rinsed the clothes in tubs of clear water, she told me something of the wide range of her experience in nursing. Maternity cases accounted for at least ninety percent of her patients, and her vivid descriptions ranked from the "pore white folks" and Negroes who knelt on the floor to give birth to their children, to the complications of a "Cessare-en" birth, made necessary by a fall that injured the mother three months before the baby was due.

She had tended mothers and babies in the poorest of colored families, and in the homes of "uppity" white folks, who were able to employ a maid and a cook, in addition to a nurse to tend the mother and baby after they returned from the hospital.

Patients with bladder disorders, cancers, nervous diseases—come what might—they were all accounted for in Mary's story which came to an abrupt halt as she dropped the last wet bundle into her clothes basket.

"Well, I'se done got these clothes washed. Now I'se got to hang 'em out," she said, as she made a hasty excursion to the kitchen for clothespins. "Good Lord, Miss, it's done twelve-thirty! When does you eat?"

"Oh, not as long as you are willing to talk," I told her. "I can eat any time."

She went out in the yard and began to sing: "Come to Jesus Now."

Looking at me, she said: "You can talk. I can hear you and ain't nobody else going to hear you."

I assured her I did not mind waiting until her work was finished.

"Just as soon as I hang these clothes out, I'se got to go down town, so you'd better ask me what you wants to know now."

She continued to hang out clothes.

"So it's my schoolin' you wants to know about now?" she asked. "I got as far as the second grade. That's how come I can't talk proper now; I didn't have enough schoolin'. I went to school in Morton's Chapel. It was a church house. Us chillun went to school there during the week, and to church and Sunday School there on Sundays.

"That's the way colored folks done in them days. Now they's got a regular schoolhouse. A blind woman come through here once and give a music singin' at that church. We paid ten cents a head to hear her sing. That was the way she had to make her livin'.

"She said her ma had fourteen chillun, seven born with sight, and seven blind. She was one of them blind ones.

"After the singing was over, she said the church was a great big Morton and a little bitty chapel, and that was sure what it was. Mr. Morton that give that chapel was one grand fine man.

"I don't hardly know how I met my husband. I believe when I met him he was with his first wife. I thought he was the prettiest man I ever seed, and he said he thought I was pretty, too.

"He told me I had the prettiest legs—they was so big. I was just a little low squat. I never seed him no more in about four years. Then he was separated from his wife. When I seed him he was on the job. I knowed his face and he knowed mine.

"Us went together about a year before our marriage. Us got

married all right, but there wasn't no big weddin', just a crowd of folks come to the house to see and hear the preacher say a little somepin' over us. Two of our four chillun is girls and the other two is boys."

Mary had finished hanging out the clothes and started in the house when a large German police dog come out of a dog house and barked at her.

"I just hates this big old dog. I wish my son-in-law would come and git him," she complained. "I has to keep him chained up so he can't run off." She spoke to the snarling animal, "Now you just go on back, because you ain't going to git none of this somepin' to eat I'se got for my hog."

Picking up a market basket of bread scraps from the yard she sat it on the porch.

"Miss, if you wants me to talk to you, you'll have to come with me in my bedroom."

I followed her through the kitchen.

"Come in here first. I wants you to see my daughter's room. She lives in Atlanta, and she's going to move her furniture when she gits a room there."

The room and its contents seemed clean but revealed no attempt at orderly arrangement. The conglomeration of its furnishings included a walnut bedroom suite which was crowded against chairs and tables of various kinds. A pink bedspread clashed with the red drapes that framed the dingy curtains at the windows, and a cheap rug, of red rose pattern, added another wide splash of color.

We went to the kitchen where a round table, surrounded by chairs in the center of the room, was easily accessible to a small wood-burning cook stove. Pots, pans, dishes, and cutlery, as well as food, were scattered around apparently at random.

Passing through a narrow hall, we entered a bathroom which

was complete with tub and other conveniences. The fixtures were cheap and crude, but they were a source of pride to Mary. She lives in a house with a bath and an indoor "lavatory."

"Nurses knows the needcessity of these things and us does without other things, but us has to have our bathrooms," she declared.

The small hall also led to a room barely large enough for a battered iron single bed and an old oak dresser.

"I stripped this bed this morning," Mary declared, "and I ain't had time to make it up yit."

The mattress tick was split its full length, exposing lumps of dingy cotton. She opened another door, saying, "Come in here. This is my bedroom."

The two iron beds in her room had evidently seen much use and many coats of paint, which was flecking off now and revealed more then one color. There was no attempt at orderly arrangement of the oak dresser, mahogany center table and its coal oil lamp, two rockers, and several split bottom chairs that were scattered about at a safe distance from the small heater.

"Have a chair and 'scuse me whilst I fixes my hair."

After several moments of vigorous wielding of the comb, she began replaiting her hair in tight braids that meandered at random about her head until the last lock of hair had been securely fastened in the braids. Few, if any, hairpins were necessary, for the hair was gathered up in such a manner that the braids did not form incipient "pigtails" but lay close against the scalp.

This chore finished, Mary said, "I'm going to git me somepin' to eat; I can't do without food as long as you can."

She returned in a short time with a plate of biscuits and stewed fruit.

"I would ask you to have some of these peaches and biscuits, but I knows you wouldn't eat nothin' like this. This here fruit ain't got a bit of sugar in it 'cause I didn't have none to sweeten it with.

"Workin' 'round doctors has done learnt me that you has to eat careful to keep well, even if you ain't got nothin' much to spend on eats. Too much bread by itself ain't good for folks, and these old peaches is got somethin' in 'em that I needs.

"'Cordin' to what I'se been told, they's better for me without no sugar no how. One of the best doctors I works for—when they's any work for me to do—ever more fusses down if he finds any of his patients that's old as I is eatin' sugar on grapefruits even. He says middle-aged folks ain't got no business stuffin' theyselfs with sweets and meats. Not that I'll ever be able to buy no more grapefruits, let alone sugar to go on 'em, unless I can git me some work to do.

"No, ma'am, us don't own this house. Us pays seven dollars a month for it. Us used to pay nine dollars a month, but times got so tight the colored woman what owns it had to cut the rent 'cause us wasn't able to pay that much. All her chillun got grown and she picked up and went off to Detroit with 'em.

"Lord knows I couldn't pay no proper rent for a place like this with a lavatory and plastered walls. I sure couldn't. I'se been livin' here five years this last gone August, long enough to own it.

"Sure, I belongs to the church. I'se a good old Baptist, I is. Why, I wasn't nothin' but a gal when I joined up with Morton's Chapel Baptist Church almost nigh thirty year ago.

"Now I knows I'se told you just about all the experiences I'se ever had, and I can't stay no longer. And this is sure 'nough: I 'spects you to gimme five cents to ride to town on the bus, 'cause I'se too tired to walk. I knows you'se obliged to be hungry, for one thing sure, you stayed right on here till you finished what you come for without nothin' to eat.

"That beats me how you done it, for I'se got to have my eats on time. It's about time for that bus. I thanks you for this nickel."

• • •

On my second trip to Mary's house, she saw me before I reached the front door.

"Just open the door and come on in," she called. "What's the use of knockin' when I'se lookin' right at you? You sure does look hot, so have that chair over there by the window. A good breeze is comin' in there.

"What'd you fetch me? Seem's like to me if the government's payin' you for this story, you oughta pay me part of what you gits outen it."

Mary was ironing. Her ironing board was resting on the backs of split-bottomed chairs. Large field rocks were placed on the seats of the chairs to keep them from tilting under the vigorous onslaught of her heavy iron. She was ironing a white uniform of the type usually worn by nurses, and did not make any further attempt to talk until the garment was carefully folded and placed across the back of a rocking chair. Then she unfolded a tightly-wadded piece that proved to be a ragged pillowcase and spread it out on the board.

"If you'se noticin' this pillow case, you might as well know it's mine, for I wouldn't wash nothing for white folks that was as ragged as this for fear they'd charge me for it, claimin' I tore it up. Colored folks has had things like that to happen, but don't ask me no questions, for I ain't goin' to tell no tales like that. They's apt to get Negroes into trouble, no matter how true they is.

"Did I tell you when you was here before that a lady that works at the college brought her washin' back to me lately after she done took it away from me and give it to somebody else? She pays me seventy-five cents a week for it now and it sure is worth ever cent of it and more besides. It tickled me for her to find out that other folks don't wash as good as I does, and besides, I just bet she had to pay more to them others she tried out.

"The most I ever got in one week was fourteen dollars, and that was on a nursin' job. I'll never forgit what the man said that hired me after my fourteen-dollar-a-week patient got to where she didn't need me no more. He didn't offer me but ten dollars a week, and I didn't want to take four dollars less than I had been gittin' and I told him so.

"'Mary,' he said, 'I don't make much myself, but whatever I promise to pay you, you'll git it and you won't have to wait for it.'

"When I goes on a job, I gives my whole time, night and day, except for four hours a day rest period, that any doctor'll tell you a nurse has gotta have if she is to stay on the job and be able to do what the patient needs her to do.

"Now you knows ten dollars a week ain't nothin' to pay for day and night services, and white folks wouldn't think of expectin' white nurses to work for such a little bit, and them white nurses does a heap less than me.

"On my last job I didn't git to take no four hours off every day, for the patient told me she couldn't stay by herself a-tall. I was on that job day and night two weeks without no extra pay for overtime. These days, nursin' jobs is so hard to git that I'se home more'n I'se off nursin'.

"I never had but three jobs of nursin' all of last year; at one I stayed two weeks, three weeks at the second, and I was on night duty six months straight at the last place. Them first two places paid me ten dollars a week, and I got a dollar a night for the night duty.

"Ellen—that's my baby gal—got as far as the eighth grade in school. She works just any place she can git a job. Most of her work's been cookin' and maidin', for that's all she knows how to do. Whenever a colored girl tries to git into some other sort of work they's always asked, 'What experience is you had?' If the new work is different from what they's been doin', they don't git it.

How's they going to git experience if nobody gives 'em a chance? Answer me that!"

"I don't know," I told her, "unless they take some sort of training for it."

"My gal ain't able to pay for that," Mary answered. "Her baby goes to the WPA nursery school, and that's a big help when I'se off nursin' and that baby's ma's off huntin' work. She almost always gits around three dollars a week when she's got work, and I reckon she might work for less if anybody would hire her. But now ain't it a shame for folks to have to work for less then it takes for 'em to live on?

"When she ain't got no work, she lives on me and her daddy; that's all she can do. Then when she does git something to do it takes all she can make to feed and clothe her and her child and to pay her part of our rent. When she ain't workin' she just mopes around here with me and her daddy.

"She ain't got no work now, and I reckon she's out huntin' a job, for she left out bright and early this mornin'.

"Our baby boy ain't married—not yit—and he's workin' his way through a school at Macon, Georgia. I don't know what he's going to take up. The school gits work for him to do. Right now they're tearing down old buildings on the campus and rebuilding 'em. My boy cleans them bricks and does anything else that comes to hand.

"I promised to provide his clothes, but I ain't been able to give him nary a garment this year, because I ain't had no money to pay for no clothes with. This is his first year off from home, and he gits mighty homesick. He writes us they don't give him enough to eat down there. You see, me being a nurse, I knows about diet and things like that and I has to know how to feed folks so as their eats will do the most good, and that's how come eatin' away from home don't satisfy none of my family.

"My oldest daughter went to the tenth grade, and since she's been out tryin' to help make a livin' she's done about everything that come to hand. She ain't never been able to give us much towards payin' for eats, and rent, and the like, for it's always took all she made to take care of her own self.

"All my chillun helps me and they daddy with the family expenses when they's home and workin', but more'n often we has to help them. But it was this oldest gal of ours I was tellin' you 'bout. She done maidin' at a big furniture and undertakin' store here and made four dollars a week as long as she could hold out at it, and lemme tell you them folks had lots of furniture for her to keep dusted and cleaned up.

"She was about the onliest one of my chillun that ever kept a steady job. Since she got married, her health's been so bad she has to stay in bed most of the time, and she don't give me one nickel no more. The doctor says she won't never be well no more till she has an operation. She ain't able to pay for that, and the Lord knows I ain't able to give it to her.

"Our oldest boy lives in this town, but he can't never seem to git nothin' much to do. He had to stop school to go to work in a drug store at one dollar a week. He's got less schoolin' than any of the others, for he never went further'n the fourth grade. His wife gits two dollars-and-a-half a week cookin' for a white woman that just keeps her half the day. She ain't borned but one child since she and our son got married, and that little boy ain't big 'nough to do nothin' but go to school yit.

"All our chillun worked every day after school was out, soon as they was big enough and could git the work to do. The girls nursed. The most I ever got from their workin' after school and all day Saturdays was a dollar-and-a-half a week apiece, but as a rule I just got a dollar apiece. I took the money and bought books, tablets, pencils, and shoes and clothes.

"School supplies wasn't furnished by the State then, and by the time I paid out for all them things, there never was enough left to dress 'em right. They always worked in vacation times if they could find the work to do. It was lots easier for 'em to find summertime work than it was in school time, for folks wanted workers that could stay all day on the job.

"Both the boys done most of they work betwixt school hours at drug stores, carryin' packages, waitin' on curb trade, and doin' all sorts of odd jobs 'bout them stores.

"When I first come to this town to live I didn't have no nursin' job, so I started out takin' in washin' for the mill folks. My prices was all accordin' to how many was in the families, about a quarter of a dollar for each person in the family. Where a family had a papa, a mama, and one child, I usually got about seventy-five cents a week, and if they was five folks in the family they had to pay me a dollar and a quarter for a week's washin'. Takin' it all in all, by and large, I'se spent more of my life washin' than nursin'. There ain't been no rest for me, only on Sundays, and not then when I'se got a nursin' job, for I has to work to feed my family.

"My husband mixes mortar. When he can git enough work to do he can make as much as five or six dollars a week, but he don't hardly ever git more'n two weeks work in any month, and oftentimes not that much. White folks won't give him no other sort of work, and no more of it—just a week or two, now and then.

"Folks is tellin' around here that the white folks is done passed a law not to work middle-age men. That may be so, but they don't give colored folks no jobs no-how, because if they would give my son a job, he could help take care of us.

"My son knows the mortar business just like his daddy; yet and still, he'll do anythin' he can find to do, but then he can't git a job.

"Now, you may not believe me, Miss, but I'se going tell you the truth: when us don't have no work to do, us just sets around here hungry. Right now my house rent is way past due, and that rentin' agent is talkin' 'bout puttin' us out iffen he don't git ten dollars to go on back rent right quick. Us used to pay our rent direct to the woman what owns the house.

"She lives in Detroit, like I done told you when you was here before. She got so tired foolin' with us gittin' behind so often and payin' in little old driblets, that she turned it over to a hard-boiled agent that'll set your things in the street in a hurry when you don't pay like he tells you to.

"We knows now we's got to git the rent cash from somewhere and give it to him on the dot.

"Right now, our water bill is on the cut-off list again, because us owes something more'n three dollars on back bills. They ain't cut it off yit, but they's apt to any minute. A notice come in the mail this mornin' from the electric light folks, sayin' iffen us don't pay that $2.66 us owes for lights they's going to cut 'em off. Well, if they does, I'll just start using my old kerosene lamp again.

"I'se tellin' you what's the truth; things is in a worser condition now than they's ever been in before, since I come on this earth. When I was first married, about thirty year ago, it wasn't no effort to step out and get a job. If things got tight in town, a person could go to the country and git work in the fields to help out.

"Now, you can't git nothin' to do in the country, for what few white folks is still runnin' farms ain't able to pay out much for wages. My cousin that lives in the country has a wife and eight chillun to bed, feed, and clothe, and he don't git but sixty cents a day.

"His wife has two little washin's. Come springtime, the chillun totes cotton seed and guano and drops corn. They chops cotton and in the fall they picks it, but none of them little jobs pays enough to pay for the clothes they rots out with sweat whilst they's doin' the work.

"It used to be almost any family could grow enough corn, wheat, potatoes, and sugar cane for syrup, to last 'em all winter. Now them folks what carries out government orders has cut down on 'em so, they don't grow enough home-raised victuals to eat.

"I will say for 'em, they ain't cut down on potatoes and other vedibles yit—just mostly corn, wheat, and sugar cane, and, oh, yes, I mustn't forgit—they's got hard-boiled about how much tobacco a man can raise. I reckon the folks that's at the tiptop head of the government knows what they's doin' when they fixes up they plans, but I don't believe they meant for the folks that carries out the orders to run things like they does.

"If things was done just like our President wants 'em done, I don't believe there'd be no hungry folks, or no folks sufferin' for lack of fire to warm by in cold weather, and no little chillun stayin' out of school, because they ain't got no clothes to wear to the schoolhouse in winter weather.

"White folks in general don't have no idea how us colored folks is sufferin'. If us was to try to carry our troubles to 'em, like us used to whenever a colored family had some white family to look to, they wouldn't listen to us now. We wouldn't git nowhere with our story, for they's got troubles of they own.

"Since freedom come, the colored folks is done come so far from what they was before the war that white folks don't feel responsible for 'em no more.

"Almost all colored folks in town tries to carry insurance to help out when they gits sick and enough to bury 'em with. I'se got one policy I pays twenty-five cents a week on. But country folks don't have no way to make extra twenty-five centses to pay on no insurance policy. It used to be they could bring chickens and eggs, vedibles, or whatever else they might have—sometimes melons and fruits—to town and swap 'em at the stores for coffee, sugar, and other things they needed.

"Now they don't have them things to bring, and if they does bring 'em, they can't swap 'em for nothin'. When a person that ain't got no insurance and no money dies, they's buried like a cat or a dog without no embalmin'. You can't expect them undertakers to do embalmin' for nothin'; it's expensive.

"When us first come to town to live, for a woman to make four dollars a week washin' was considered big money. It took a heap of work to make that much; I knows, 'cause I done it.

"My husband worked for the city till he fell off of one of them city trucks and broke his collar bone. After he got well they wouldn't take him back, even if he did git hurt doin' they work just like they told him to. Up to the time of his fall he was makin' nine dollars a week, but since that time he makes whatever folks is minded to pay him.

"Let me tell you the God's truth! Since 1932, lots of colored folks has died hungry. Look! See how big this dress hangs on me. I've lost ten pounds, and every pound of it was lost because I didn't have enough to eat. I'll be glad if I ever see the day again when I can put my foots under somebody's table and eat a belly full one more time.

"Not long ago I asked a white woman why colored folks couldn't git no work to do. She told me the Negro race had brought it on theyselfs. She said that when times was good and white folks would go to hire a cook or a nurse they would be told: 'Us ain't workin' out no more. Us is lookin' for a cook, a washerwoman, or a nurse ourselfs.'

"She say our sassy ways like that is why the white folks don't pay us no more heed since times is done got so tight they ain't no jobs for us.

"It ain't been long since I asked a white woman to loan me five dollars to help me out of a awful tight. She lied when she told me with a straight face that she just didn't have it. I knowed she did have it because some of her folks had just died and left her a sight of money. The only way she could make me believe she ain't got it now would be to git the Good Lord to come down as a natural man, and tell me she ain't got that much money she don't need that she could loan me. One thing sure, these folks that's got so much can't take none of it with 'em.

"So all right, I say, let 'em keep they old money.

"Say, listen, now ain't the government got some sort of office in town where they can loan out money to help pore folks to git back on they foots after they's done got down and out? No, I don't mean no Rural Rehab's business; I means just a straight out loan?

"Well, iffen you don't know about it, I don't expect they's no such place here; but if they was, they sure would do a big heap of business.

"A little flour and a very little coffee is all they is in this house to eat today. Soon as I gits the seventy-five cents for this washin,' I aims to take it and buy us some meat. My husband ain't had but one day's work this week and he won't git no pay befo' Saturday, and that day's work don't come to but a dollar.

"The older doctors used to look out for us practical nurses, but these younguns what's doin' the doctorin' now don't do that no more. And I liked the ways the older doctors had of lookin' after sick folks lots better'n I does the young doctor's ways. Before one of them old-time doctors would leave, they'd ask you lots of questions about how you meant to handle the patient till they found how much you knowed. And then they'd tell you how in such a nice way that it seemed like they was just offerin' suggestions, but you knowed better'n to fail to do what they suggested.

"These here young doctors rushes in and out like bats out of torment, and before you knows it they's gone without tellin' you nothin'. Yet, if anything goes wrong it's sure to be all your fault. They ain't quite all of the youngsters that bad. I worked for one young doctor here last year that advised with me plenty and always asked me questions till he was satisfied I knowed how to treat his patient.

"Take them old doctors; when one of them come to see a patient and saw he was sufferin', he always give somethin' to ease the pain if it was needed. These here younguns just stays long enough to take the temperature, feel the pulse, and tell the nurse to slap an ice-cap on the patient's head till the ambulance can git there to take him to the hospital. Then the pore nurse is left without no job, and the patient is feeling the expense of a operation. Gimme them good old doctors—do you hear me? —any day in the week.

"When a doctor takes a patient that's got money to the hospital, he's charged like '30 going North,' but if sick folks and they families ain't got nothin', the charges is sometimes reasonable enough for operations and sich like. I ain't never had to pay for none of them things for myself, because I ain't never been to no hospital to be cut nowheres, and I hopes I never will have to go.

"I known I asked you the last time you was here, but, Miss, in all your gittin' around and talkin' to so many folks, don't you never hear of no job you could point out to me? I ain't only a good nurse and a washerwoman, but I can cook good, too. I don't like cookin', but I can do it, and do a fine job of it, if I do say so my own self. One thing sure, I ain't able to do no more big heavy washin's like I used to, but if I can't git me nothin' else to do I'll have to git another small washin'. Now, why don't you lemme try your washin'? I knows you'd like the way I does washin' and ironin'.'"

Remembering how often I had seen her spit on the clothes when I was taking her first interview, I hastily told Mary that mine was a heavy washing, for my children in school needed so many clothes that it would be too much of a burden on her.

"You sure don't need me to tell you no more," she grumbled, "for I'se done told you all I ever did know, and besides I'se hungry now and I wants to hurry through this ironin' so I can go after my money and git me somepin to eat."

Recognizing her intention to end the conversation, I gathered up my notes and prepared to leave.

"If you ever does have to come back, tell them government folks you works for to send me some money for this talkin' I'se done for you."

As I started out of her room, Mary said, "Excuse me, Miss, for not stoppin' to go to the door with you, but I can't play with this here electric iron, like I could them old flat irons us used to heat on charcoal buckets."

She stuck a finger in her mouth and then applied it to the iron. I could hear the sizzle of the spittle, which proved to her that the iron was hot enough to work on starched clothes. I thanked her and left. She called after me, "Don't you forget to write it down straight that I ain't no midwife yet. They puts folks in jail that says they's midwifes and can't show no 'stificate."

The Atlanta Life Insurance Company
꤇꒢꒜꤇

Editor's Note: John H. Roberson, listed as J. H. "Robertson" in Mrs. Grace McCune's interview manuscript, was the manager of the Athens office of the Atlanta Life Insurance Company, called the "Capital City Insurance Company" in the interview. Atlanta Life was founded by Alonzo Franklin Herndon, a former slave, and today Atlanta Life has assets of more than $200 million and operates in seventeen states. The Athens office was in the Samaritan Building, two doors down from the Morton Building. The Samaritan Building was torn down for a parking lot.

John Roberson was not listed in the 1938 Athens City Directory, but he was in the 1940 directory, living at 760 N. Chase St. He was also in the 1942 directory, but not in later directories. I have not found any information about his other residence locations or when he died.

• • •

The young Negress, who sat at her desk in the reception room of the Atlanta Life Insurance Company's local office, was industriously thumbing through a sheaf of papers when I entered. She stood up at once when she saw me, and when I expressed a desire to talk with the manager of the office, she said, "Just have a seat, and I'll see if he is busy."

As she left me to open a door marked "PRIVATE," I noticed her straightened hair, combed back from her face and arranged in a smooth coil on the back of her head. Her neatly fitted frock was made on the tailored lines of appropriate office costuming for women. She returned promptly, saying, "Mr. Roberson will see you now."

She led the way, and on entering the small private office I saw a young Negro man dressed in an impeccably tailored and freshly pressed dark blue business suit.

"I'm J. H. Roberson," he greeted me, standing beside his desk, "What can I do for you?"

He laughed when I asked him to relate some of his experiences and problems in his occupation as an insurance man.

"We do have a good many problems," he admitted, "And our experiences might fill a good many books. But first, won't you have a seat?"

"Tell me about your early life," I asked.

"Well," he said, "I was born in a small town in South Georgia, in 1905. The folks down there may not consider it so small—they even have a daily paper there—but after spending so many years in Atlanta and Athens, and visiting other larger cities, I came to realize that I am from a small town. My father worked at sawmills and consequently was away from home much of the time, for when one lot of timber was cut, the sawmill had to be moved to another tract.

"One of my earliest recollections is my determination to earn money. I wanted to have my own money and to be independent. I hardly know just how old I was when I began work as a boot-black. It's really surprising how many nickels and dimes a small boy can earn blacking shoes.

"During my grammar school days, I was on the lookout for any little chore by which I could earn money between school hours. After finishing grammar school in Moultrie, I began high school studies at Americus Institute in Americus, Georgia, but after one school year there I went to Morehouse College, in At-

The Samaritan Building, housing the Atlanta Life Insurance
Company Athens office, on Washington Street near the Morton
Theatre. *Photo credit:* Jeff Weinberg Postcard Collection

lanta, where I completed high school, and I remained there until I graduated from college.

About twenty percent of the students at Morehouse did part-
time work to earn some of their expenses. I was one of that
group, and I also began the fall term every year with quite a tidy
sum saved from wages and tips paid me at summer resorts during the vacation period.

"I waited on tables, did bellboy service, or 'most anything that
came to hand at summer hotels. When I finished college, my
plans were already definite. I wanted to go in the insurance business, for I could think of no other field that offered as promising
opportunities to a young man of my race.

"I didn't step out of college into a high-salaried executive job.

My first work was the humblest that this business has to offer. I was an agent's helper. That means I made the rounds with the agent to keep up with the literature that was distributed for advertising and selling insurance. I wasn't allowed to do any collecting, and neither could I try to sell any insurance until I was promoted to the job of assistant agent.

"Even then I was given long and careful training by the agent before I was permitted to discuss any matter of collection or selling with a policyholder or a sales prospect. It takes someone who is plenty interested in insurance to stick through the long training period.

"I can tell you it was hard on me during my first experience in trying to keep up the quota required of all agents and their assistants. There were days when it seemed impossible to make even a small increase in the volume of sales and collections. I would have given up then, but I very well knew it was only by means of bringing in more business than the other agents that I could hope for promotion, and I was firmly determined to get it.

"The agent with me knew I was doing my very best and that I wanted, more than anything else in the world, to make good at insurance work, so he did everything in his power to encourage and assist me. It was his kindness and understanding that enabled me to successfully pass through the trying period of training.

"When dark came, the other agents would call it a day, and they would go out for an evening of pleasure and frolicking around at dances and shows, but I worked right on. That was my time for contacting those of our people who couldn't be reached in the daytime because of their jobs. It was this night work that enabled me to pile up a higher total of insurance sold than the others in my district, and eight years ago it won me my place as manager.

"Now we have a regular training school for young men of

twenty-one and over who want to enter the insurance business. We take twenty or thirty of them and start training the group. They don't have to have college education for this work, for we teach them according to our own ideas. Do you know that some of the best executives in the insurance business are men that never finished high school? Some of the top-notchers never even finished grammar school.

"Education is a great thing, but that old school of experience beats 'em all, because that's where you have to work for yourself. That's one school that will make you put out all there is in you.

"We start our agents off with small salaries, plus a commission on all business above a certain quota. That's an incentive to work, because they realize that the amount of their earnings depends on their own efforts and resourcefulness, and they usually dig in and get the business.

"After an agent is appointed and his territory assigned he becomes responsible for the business in that definite area; not for just one type of policy but for all the different kinds of insurance that we write. All the special problems that arise in that particular territory—and believe me, there are plenty of problems coming up all the time in any territory—the agent is expected to settle by himself as far as possible. It seems as if a week never passes that some policyholder doesn't let a policy lapse for one reason or another. The agent who keeps in sufficiently close touch with his policyholders to be able to persuade them to let no insurance lapse is considered exceedingly good and is in sure line for promotion. Sometimes the lapses will total more than the new business, and that's when we get discouraged and feel like giving up.

"Of course we investigate every risk as well as we can before we write the insurance, and then do more investigating before we pay any claim that appears to be in the least doubtful, but even at that we do get caught sometimes.

"Things aren't always as they appear on the surface and it's not possible to accurately judge the physical condition by casual inspection of outward appearances. People who want to collect on sick benefit claims will swear to anything that they think they can get by with.

"When they want to get a policy written, they'll swear they have never had to see a doctor, at least not for the last five or ten years. All the time they're just planning to cash in on some disease already present in their bodies and which they may be able to conceal from us long enough to get the insurance written and in effect.

"We've learned that there are almost as many speculators as there are honest people. This is especially so on the sick and accident policies. Some of our policies carry sick benefits that run as high as twenty-five dollars a week, and persons have tried to collect as soon as the policy was in force. Then again we have had some that have carried these policies for years, and have never put in for the first claim.

"I'll never forget the time when a woman who held one of our sick and accident policies, paying five dollars a week in the event she was confined to bed, tried to swindle us. We paid the first week's claim without hesitancy after I had personally visited the home and found her in bed apparently very ill.

"When the claim for a second week came in, I made my formal visit of investigation at an hour when she did not expect me. I suspected there was some reason for the excessive delay in permitting me to enter the home. I noticed the cover pulled up closely about her neck on that sweltering July day—probably to conceal the fact that she had gotten into bed fully dressed. I remained by the bedside administering simple remedies and sympathizing with the patient until the limit of her endurance was reached.

"That was after I had awkwardly mixed up quantities of freshly ironed clothes with piles of un-ironed garments and accidentally dropped them on the floor and trampled on them. I directed a neighbor woman to apply hot water bottles to the feet of the patient and mustard plasters to her chest.

"She rose up out of bed, fully clothed, even to her shoes, and said she did not want that five dollars a week if she had to go through all that to get it. But you know, I don't believe she ever did suspect anything other than that I was just extremely solicitous about her.

"That story spread through the district and it gave me a good reputation for looking after the sick people who hold insurance with me. If anyone else in that district ever tried to swindle me in a sick benefit claim, I never did find it out.

"Now don't get the idea that we're reluctant about paying just claims. We very readily pay all just and honest claims, but because of the great number of speculators who are always ready to take any and every advantage of us, we must at all times be very careful in our investigations of claims.

"The worst feature of it all is that these speculators sometimes find doctors low enough to help them in their efforts to swindle life insurance companies. However, I'm happy to say that this doesn't happen very often.

"We always learn when these cases do show up, that the policyholder has promised to divide the benefits with the doctor when, and if, the claim is paid. I don't think they ever gain by this practice in the long run, for if they win once they invariably keep on trying to work the same gag, and sooner or later it makes a lot of trouble for them, if not a jail term."

"Are all your insurance payments weekly?" I asked.

"In town, yes; or that is, most of it is paid by the week in town. It can be paid by the month by special arrangement. Out in communities where we don't keep an agent all the time, we send a representative once a month to make collections.

"It's counted a serious matter to risk loss of money by letting insurance lapse. Perhaps our greatest collection problem in rural communities lies in the frequency with which our policyholders move from one farm to another, and we've never been able to make them understand the importance of notifying us whenever they plan to move.

"Some of them move about so much. They will stay probably a year on one farm and then get dissatisfied for some reason. Usually they think they haven't been treated right, didn't get enough pay, or the people they rented from didn't advance them enough during the year to get by with their bills until the crop was sold.

"Sometimes it's the illness or death of the main breadwinner in a family that's the reason for the move, but they scarcely ever stay in one place over a year or two at the most, for they're always thinking they can do better at some other place.

"Sometimes they move into a county where they're not known, and it's a problem to locate them then. I've known it to take several months to locate one policyholder. They just don't cooperate with the agent. After all that work in locating them, when we ask, 'Why didn't you let us know where you had moved?' we get this answer, 'I just never thought about it.'"

He laughed and continued, "But you know that's about the truth of the matter—they just don't think; that's one great fault of my people.

"I don't know if you know this or not, but one of the greatest mistakes our people make is when they let a policy lapse, they'll sometimes just drop that one and take out a new policy with another agent. I've known this to happen many times, and I've occasionally known them to die before the new policy is in force.

"If they had only kept the old policy in effect by keeping it paid up, they would have received its value. It's hard to make them understand this.

"People with high incomes don't need insurance like those who work on small, uncertain salaries. I really don't know just what my people would do in some emergencies without their insurance, for it's one thing on which they can depend.

"Take the washwomen, cooks, maids, and all the others that work for two and three dollars a week. What do they have to depend on? Their earnings are not even enough for the necessities of living, and if sickness should come, they couldn't get a doctor to come unless he knew he would get his money, and it's the same in case of death.

"They'd have to lay out until enough money was raised to pay burial expenses. But if they have a good insurance policy they can get the doctor to come, and if they should pass on, the doctor, as well as the undertaker, would get his money.

"Yes, a good policy is something they can depend on, and if they can possibly get the money to keep it in force, they won't knowingly let it lapse.

"Another feature of insurance which has brought up many questions and caused some lawsuits is the minor-child beneficiary. Of course, we can't turn the money over to a child, and sure as the world when the uncles and aunts of the beneficiary learn that the child has money coming from insurance, they all fall out about who is to be the guardian.

"Each one of them will want the child as long as they expect it to receive money. In most of these instances we have turned the money over to a court, whose duty it was to appoint a guardian for the child and its money.

"Today we refuse to write policies that name children as beneficiaries unless the policyholder specifies a guardian in the application for the policy.

"As to the matter of production, we divide the business area into districts, and in each district we set up a local office in some central town. The personnel of the local office include manager, assistant manager, cashier, clerk, inspectors, supervisors, and agents. Each supervisor has from four to six agents working under him.

"While we understand that not every prospect called on will take out insurance, we do expect our agents to land at least three out of every ten they call on. Each agent has his prospect book, and in this is kept the names of all the people he calls on, the date of each call, and a notice of when he expects to see each prospect again. Sometimes it takes weeks for the agent to make just one trip to each of his prospects, but whether they want him or not, he hunts them up and calls regularly, just as a matter of persistence.

"Do you know that in the end these regular calls usually win out for the agent?

"Few people on the outside realize the valuable services we render to morticians. You know the collection end of their business is bound to be difficult, for they are compelled to bury the deceased even if they never get anything for their services and merchandise.

"As a usual thing, people are inclined to request expensive funerals for their relatives, whether they can pay the bills or not. We encourage the proprietors of undertaking establishments to call us as soon as they are notified of a death, so that we can let them know whether or not the deceased has insurance with us.

"Most of the other insurance companies extend the same courtesies. When they know in advance how much cash will be available, the morticians are enabled to make a more sensible deal with the family. They can show only what they know can be paid for.

"It's an established fact that unless they get at least a substantial part of the cost before the interment, it will be difficult for them to collect at all. After they have rendered services to the best of their ability, furnished burial robes and casket, and used their hearse, automobiles and other equipment, there is little that they can do toward collection after the body is under the ground.

"They had better get a claim on what insurance exists before they even start to work on the corpse.

"We don't have very much time for recreation, and there's very little in that way to do here, but our agents usually go in for whatever amusements are popular in their territories, for it's a good policy to mix with the local people. That helps business.

"We don't have any ball teams among our workers, as is customary in many other organizations, but that's because we don't know all the time where we will be located.

"Personally, I have very little time for recreation. I do enjoy swimming and billiards, also a good game of tennis in the late afternoons, and I think we all like a good picture show. I visit all the churches very often and attend their different entertainments, for, as I told you, I consider it a good policy to mix with people. Though I'm a Baptist myself, our policyholders belong to different churches, and it makes them feel better to know that we want to be with them.

"I married an Alabama girl soon after I came here to work as a manager. I have no children, and just a short time ago—it really seems ages—I lost my wife. Since she passed away, I'm left without any family.

"I get lonesome, for we were so happy, but I know that I'll have to go on some way and I'm trying to take it as she would have me to. I'm glad I stay so busy that I don't have time to brood and worry so much.

"There are so many problems of our people, and many have tried to find their solutions. The white folks are working on these things now, and I hope and believe that at some time in the near future there will be better understanding between the races.

"The South is the home of the Negro, and our people are beginning to realize it more and more in every way. Of course, some of them, in fact a great many, have gone North and have made a success of their work at the better salaries paid there. But after all, that doesn't mean so much, for it takes all they can make to live up there.

"Housing conditions can be blamed for many of the problems of my race. Our agents have found that these conditions are worse in small towns and rural areas than in the more thickly settled sections. Rain comes in through leaky roofs and they can't keep the cold out. Continued exposure in cold, wet, and unsanitary living quarters brings a notable increase in pulmonary disorders. Pneumonia flourishes in areas where these conditions prevail. In fact, the majority of our sick claims are based on this disease.

"As a general thing, there is a trend toward improvement of housing conditions throughout the section of the country that I frequent. Our people are beginning to take advantage of the plans offered by various government bureaus for financing improvement of houses. Marked improvement in rural areas is coming from the aid and encouragement now given tenant farmers toward purchase of farms and building of farm homes.

"Our company sponsors lectures and assemblies for teaching improvement of health by means of diet. We began this several years ago when an amazing number of sick benefit claims, based on varying degrees of prostration accompanied by a peculiar roughening of the skin, came in from a section in South Georgia.

"We investigated and found this malady to be pellagra. Our workers in that territory concentrated their efforts on convincing the sufferers of the benefits to be gained by properly varied diets to such an extent that we think more cures were effected by the change of food habits than by medicines.

"By means of the county agents, nursing projects, and other facilities, the government has done splendid service in teaching the essentials of proper diet to the people of your race and mine.

"It would probably be hard for you to believe what we found to be the main obstacle in our efforts to help pellagra victims in the area I've just mentioned," he remarked.

"Go ahead and tell about it," I urged. "It should be known."

"Well," he continued, lowering his voice until I had to lean forward to catch the words that followed, "In this area, almost every landlord would forbid the tenant to plant a garden for his own use, saying, 'I want you to put all of your time on your crop, so I'll plant a garden big enough to feed every family on this plantation. You plant your crop on every foot of land I've rented you.'

"So the tenant had no garden, no potato patch, no watermelon patch, no chickens, and no hogs or cows. Sure enough, the landlord would plant a grand garden, but everything the tenant used from it was charged to his account at a price that enabled the landlord to make an excellent profit. It usually left the tenant in debt to his landlord at the end of the year if he used anything from that garden.

"So the poor tenant learned to do without vegetables, milk, and fresh meats. He lived chiefly on cornbread, syrup, and fatback, and consequently became susceptible to pellagra.

"Some of our people in certain sections still find themselves hampered by restrictions like that, and so they keep moving from place to place. They're trying to get away from such things.

"Most of us can remember the time when people of my race had few opportunities for higher education. Now we have excellent high schools and colleges, as well as much improved facilities for grade school education. If young people of my race want to be educated, there is nothing to prevent them from going ahead and getting whatever training they desire.

"I'm proud or these educational institutions, for they have been the means of giving us better preparation for our work. Even the cooks need to know how to read and write, and the same knowledge enables the maid to answer your telephone more intelligently and take down the messages that come for you in your absence.

"Nursemaids give better service in the care of your children when they are trained for their work. In fact, there is no line of work—no matter now humble the service—that cannot be improved by even a little education.

"The relationship between our people and the white folks in the South is on a sounder basis than in the North. I know that many thoughtless things have been done, and some of them have been terrible in their effects on the harmony of the races.

"These things have made hardships for the rest of us. We are working in cooperation with the good white people to prevent such things from recurring, and it will all be straightened out eventually. It takes lots of time to solve problems concerning the human race, and much more time to work out those solutions sufficiently to see improvement.

"Only the Negroes who have means can make money and progress in the North. The ones that have nothing can't get along. I know many who couldn't live in the North. Eventually they'll all want to come back to the South where the majority of them were born. The South is their home. Here they have their own friends, relatives, churches, and schools. If they can just learn to get ahead, then they'll be on the road to greater advantages.

"I know many that sold their farms and moved to the North because they thought they couldn't make a go of it on the farm. They didn't know how to do much of anything except to raise cotton and corn. Now there's no excuse for the farmer not to make a good living if he's willing to work. The government has all these farm projects and agents to teach them what to plant and how to cultivate the ground to the best advantage.

"They are learning that cotton is not the reliable money crop they once thought it was. They know there are many other crops that will bring in more money, without the work and risk of one-crop farming.

"They are getting along better, having more to eat and wear then ever before on the farms. The government has really been a blessing to the farmers, yet many of them can't, or rather just won't, admit it.

"It isn't just teaching them to till the soil that counts. The agents are showing them how they can make money raising cattle for the market as well as for their own use. In this way they no longer have to depend on one crop for cash, and that keeps them from getting discouraged so easily.

"What political party do I belong to?"

An honestly puzzled expression came over his face that was quickly followed by another expansive smile, as he confessed, "I don't know. I was reared in a family of Republicans without knowing very much more about that party than the story that President Lincoln was a member of it and that he became a martyr soon after he signed the document that sealed our emancipation.

"It seemed natural to us that there was no better way for Negroes to pay tribute to the man who gave us our freedom than to vote his way, and there was no other party that seemed as much interested in our welfare as the Republicans did.

"Since the present Mr. Roosevelt was first elected, his remarkable achievements have made me do some serious thinking. I'm reluctant to vote against the old party, but I cannot ignore the fact that my people have had more consideration from the present administration than from any in the past.

"Please don't ask how I'll vote in 1940. I really don't know. I admire our President," he said.

"You've probably heard of our Mr. Herndon, the remarkable man who founded our company," he said, looking up at a large framed photograph.

"Everyone has heard of him, and I can very well remember seeing him—for I passed his barber shop in Atlanta almost every day, about 30 years ago," I replied, "But I'd like to hear his story from you."

"Well," Roberson continued, "He was born a slave, in Monroe County, Georgia. After freedom came, he went to Atlanta and started to work for a barber. That he made a success of his work is shown by the large business he built up.

"His best customers were among his white friends. Before 1900 his barber shop had more then 20 chairs in it, and that shop is still going today, long after his death. A list of his patrons would sound like a roll call of Atlanta's most prominent and important businessmen.

"It may be that his daily contact with successful businessmen had something to do with his own success. His ambition to do something to enable the members of our race to prepare for the financial crises so often brought about by sickness, accidents, and by death, led him to organize his first little accident and sick benefit company.

"It's probable that the purity and unselfishness of his motives in starting his insurance business were factors that led Providence to permit it to prosper. In 1905 he was able to buy out several other companies, organize a great business, and put up a $5,000 cash bond in accordance with a law enacted that year by the State Legislature for the protection of insurance beneficiaries.

"Prior to that time, there had been several small companies doing business in accident and sick benefit insurance that carried death benefits of from twenty to thirty dollars, and not one of these little organizations was able to raise the cash bond. Mr. Herndon's purchase of these small companies and merging them with his original insurance business was the beginning of the Atlanta Life Insurance Company, and our home offices are still in Atlanta.

"Our little mutual company, that before the merger in 1905 paid sick benefits of from two to three dollars a week, has grown and improved until we have more than 300,000 policyholders, and we're now one of the largest insurance organizations among our people. We write any kind of insurance now, from sick, accident, straight life, and paid-up, to endowment. In fact, this is an industrial as well as an ordinary life insurance company, and we're more than proud of our business.

"Our records show that in 1939 we paid out more than $800,000 to our paid-up policyholders and to beneficiaries in general. This, of course, includes loans on policies, sick and accident benefits, dividends, and final payments after the death of the insured.

"After making these payments totalling considerably more than three-quarters of a million dollars, we still had a surplus of more than $980,000 on hand. At the beginning of this year we raised the amount of capital stock from $100,000 to $500,000.

"Our 104 employees include our managers, clerks, inspectors, and field agents. That'll give you some idea of how our business has grown."

There was a proud and satisfied look on his face when he asked, "Now do you like our new home?"

As I looked about, he continued, "We've just recently moved

into these offices. We'd simply outgrown the old place and just had to have more room."

The modern offices were well furnished and equipped. Venetian blinds shaded the windows facing the street, and the walls and woodwork were immaculate in their fresh coats of light tan paint.

"You have every reason to be proud of these lovely offices," I assured him, "And they have the advantage of being centrally located and convenient for your workers and clients."

"Thank you," he answered, "Now I think I've just about covered everything of interest about my insurance experience. I don't have to explain that practically my whole scheme of living is bounded by insurance now. There is no other business that I know of that brings the worker in such close contact with the great mass of our race as does insurance, and through it we are able to have insight into the most personal problems.

"While a child to still very young, some insurance man is going to be there to see about writing a policy on its life. An insurance man will investigate practically every condition that effects the health and welfare of his policyholder throughout his life, and when he has died, the insurance man comes around again to make settlement.

"Everything that the insurance man does to improve health conditions and to take care of his policyholder is actually an economy for he is lessening the payments of sickness and death claims. But I still maintain that our Mr. Herndon founded this business for the purpose of helping the people of his race.

"I'm hoping that you'll find at least a part of the information I've given you usable. If in the future there are questions that arise in regard to our race, I hope that you'll let us try to help you compile the information needed."

The Successful Farmer

The family of James Lewis McLeroy was an early-day family in the Watkinsville and Athens areas early in the nineteenth century. James McLeroy, the subject of this interview, was born June 22, 1857, in Watkinsville, the son of Frances Marion and Elizabeth Lester McLeroy. Sadie B. Hornsby interviewed him Aug. 8, 1939 at his home at 295 Oglethorpe Ave., Athens. She incorrectly identified him as James L. McElroy, but Mrs. Henry Grady McLeroy, Jr., of Athens, has identified him as James Lewis McLeroy.

• • •

Mr. McLeroy was sitting at his desk in the front hall near the door engaged in thumbing over one paper after another. The papers were evidently of importance and pertaining to his business affairs, for some he lingered over longer than others. It was obvious that he was so absorbed in his task that he didn't hear my approach to the front porch, for when I knocked on the door it startled the old man, and he jumped as if something unexpected had happened.

Mr. McLeroy is tall and portly, with white hair, faded blue eyes, and a face which is criss-crossed with wrinkles and deeply tanned and roughened by the sun, wind, and rain of eighty-two years. His gray, shaggy eyebrows hang over his silver-rimmed glasses.

It was an effort for him to get up from the chair as he is badly crippled in his right leg from the waist down. He hobbled to the door saying, "Good morning," and before I had a chance to state my mission he added, "Now if it's something you want to sell, young woman, I'm not interested, and don't have the money to invest in anything. I don't read much now, for I can't see good like I used to."

After I had explained the object of my visit, he invited me in.

"Come in, won't you, or had you rather sit on the porch? But if it's all the same to you we'll sit here in the hall, 'cause the sun hurts my eyes. You'll have to excuse the house; the woman folks are cleaning house and have everything torn up."

There was a loud noise in the back of the house, and asking to be excused a minute, he called out, "Sue, are you moving the Frigidaire? You go careful. If you jar some of the electrical parts loose it will cost me several dollars to have it fixed." The noise stopped and a Negro boy and an older Negro went into a room down the hall and came out carrying an old-fashioned dresser.

Mr. McLeroy said to the woman who made her appearance about that time, "What in tarnation are you going to do with that dresser?"

"Taking it up the stairs," she replied.

"What for?" he wanted to know.

"Because there is no sense having two dressers in one room, and there is nothing else up there."

Nothing more was said and he resumed his conversation.

"Now, just to tell you the truth, I don't know anything about legends connected with Athens or any place near by. All I ever heard connected with Athens was when the Yankees came through. A man, who was in the crowd at that time, told me when the Yankees came through here a band of them began to steal everything they could get their hands on, as well as molested the women and children. Our boys caught the ringleader of the gang, hung him up by his thumbs in a clump of woods on the other side of town, and the others got away."

I heard the one he called Sue call, "Sister Ruth, have you put your vacuum cleaner up?"

"No."

"Well, let me use it for a while."

"All right, go in my room and get it."

The noise from the cleaner began in the room the dresser was removed from. Mr. McLeroy called in a sharp voice, "Sue, cut that blame thing off. I can't hear a word this lady has to say."

There was no response, and the noise continued. He got up from his chair, hobbled into the room, and closed the door. The noise within ceased. He seemed embarrassed over the condition of the torn-up house, as there was a conglomeration of furniture throughout the full length of the hall—many old-fashioned chairs, sofas, tables, and what not. Through an open door in what appeared to be the dining room, I saw an old square dining table with a lovely crocheted cloth on it.

My host returned and sat down in a large rocker, after he had stopped the noise and confusion.

"Now, where do you want me to begin? Would you like to know about my father first? Well, he was a famous Baptist preacher. He served as pastor for a number of churches for years. Some of them he preached at as long as twenty-five years, hand running.

"I was born at Watkinsville, in Clarke County then but Oconee County now, on June 21, 1857. My father left Watkinsville when I was quite a child. He moved out here about a quarter of a mile on Mitchell's Bridge Road. My father owned a large gin and grist mill. He ginned cotton and ground corn into meal for everybody around Athens. I know one thing I did as a boy. I have hauled hundreds of bushels of corn in winter right by this very house in those days when the road was a foot deep in mud.

"The corn was ground between two huge stones pulled around

James Lewis McLeroy. *Photo credit:* Mr. and
Mrs. Henry Grady McLeroy, Jr.

and round by mules or horses. Now all that is done by electric-
ity and the meal is ground by wheels pulled by belts connected to
the grinder.

"When I was a boy I had to walk four miles to school every day,
four there and four back, making eight miles a day. Now children
can't walk up here several blocks to college. I went to school here
in Athens to a private school for boys, taught by Mr. Scudder. The
school in recent years has been converted into a dwelling house.
It is standing on the original spot, next to the First Presbyterian
Church. After I finished there, which took me three years, I went

to another private school taught by Sylvanus Morris and Judge Lumpkin. I went there three years. Among other subjects I took was bookkeeping. I have never used it only in my own business. That old school stood where the Fowler house is now, and was recently bought by a fraternity.

"The school I went to was a residence converted into a schoolhouse and was known at that time as the Old Charbonnie [Charbonnier] House. Schools wan't as good in those days as they are now, and that was the last place I went to school. I didn't go to college. It took a heap of money to go to college back in my young days.

"Yes, mam, I have been here a long time. Why, I remember when there wan't nothing but houses on Clayton Street, with the exception of where Sun's Drug Store is now and there was a blacksmith shop. And I have seen mud half a leg deep on Broad Street after a heavy rain. I remember when the first paving was laid, but of course I don't remember the year, as my mind is too short now to recall the exact year.

"I helped my father on the farm and at the cotton gin until I was twenty-one years of age, doing everything that came to hand, working on the farm in season and at the cotton gin and grist mill in the fall and winter.

"When I became a 'free' man I married and went to farming for myself. I still farm, but it is run by tenant labor. I've been very successful handling labor. One Negro family has been on my farm twenty-five years and another has been with me twenty-three. I have a twenty-five horse farm; therefore, I have several other families living on it. The cotton gins are quite different now from what they were when I was a boy. The old ones were fed by hand.

"After my father died, I moved to town. A man had bought and built this house. He also owned two lots next to this one. Times got tight with him and he came near losing his property and this house he lived in at the time. I bought this property from him, which caused him to get on his feet and start all over again. That was twenty-seven years ago.

"When I moved to town I built a modern gin, grist mill, and shingle mill, also a feed mill. I have ginned as high as three thousand bales of cotton in one season, but the Government has cut the cotton acreage down so my boys didn't gin but a little better than six hundred bales last year. The report on cotton is it seems much larger than last year.

"I have been nearly killed several times fooling around the cotton gin. When I was running a water pipe to the gin, I had to connect it with the water main over here at the Co-ordinate College. Of course I had secured permission from the proper authorities. You have to be careful that the pipes are free of dirt, so I picked up a long pipe to knock the dirt out before the men working on the main laid it. In doing so I struck a pipe and it knocked me flat on the ground senseless.

"One day while working around the gin, the cuff of my shirt caught on a line shaft and went around for some time before the machinery could be stopped and I was pulled out. Every stitch of clothing was torn from my right side but the cuff of my shirt. My hip was badly mangled and it was thought for a long time I would never walk again without the aid of crutches. I was about fifty-five years old when that happened.

"I told you that I ran a shingle mill in connection with my cotton gin. Do you see my hand, with the two fingers gone? Well, let me tell you how it happened. I had an emery wheel attached to the machinery on my shingle mill. I had just finished whetting a saw. I noticed the shingles were backing up, and very carefully I reached my hand down between the saws to scatter the shingles. When I pulled my hand out it was in some way knocked up against the saw. It sawed two fingers off in less than a second, and they flew out and hit the wall about ten feet from me.

"W-e-l-l, it's like this, what I made on my gin, grist, and shingle mill, has enabled me to buy what property I cared to own. I fed, clothed, educated, and gave my children a few opportunities those times could afford. I have started each of my ten children out in business. I think that is evidence of what the success of the gins and farm has been.

"I was the father of thirteen children, but only eleven of them lived to be grown and married. One of my daughters died soon after her first child was born, and the child died a few weeks later, but her husband is dead now.

All of my children have a high school education, and four or five of them finished college. The rest of them wouldn't go. My wife and I were married sixty-one years before her death. She died this past December, and my oldest child will be sixty years old his next birthday.

"My widowed daughter and her little boy are living with me now, sorter keeping things together for me. But I am going to get married again just as soon as I can find some nice lady that will have me. You don't know a nice woman about fifty or sixty who would like a nice home and a good husband? If you do, tell them about me. If I married again my children would have a fit, but I don't see why, because as fast as their wives or husbands died, they were ready to get them somebody else.

"Due to my father being a Baptist preacher, naturally all of us belong to the Baptist church, and so to speak I was born in the church. Rain or shine, snow or blow, that is one thing my father demanded of us. My mother made preparations on Saturday, and bright and early Sunday morning, if it was a country church my father served and it was a good distance from home, we set forth to be there on time."

The telephone rang, and the young woman he called Sue answered. Then she called to Mr. McLeroy, "Papa, hurry and come on. Maybelle is waiting on us."

He said to me, "Everything is so torn up here today, one of my daughters has invited us to have dinner with her. I am sorry to have to go, but you know when a woman gets a meal ready, it makes them mad to keep 'em waiting.

"Suppose you go by the gin on the way to town and look the gin over. But, before you go, I want to show you something I picked up in the field on my farm. Here it is. I used it for a paper weight all these years. Some people tell me it looks like a pine cone petrified. It does resemble one, but the sections that form the burr are diamond shaped and clear as crystal. Some of my folks took ink and traced around each of the sections that form the burr.

"I meant to take it down town and have it cleaned, but I have never gotten around to it. Here is a rock I found. It looks like it was shaped by an expert. I have found many arrow-heads, pots, and things in days gone by left by the Indians. I have often been sorry my wife let the children break them.

"It has always puzzled me what the Indians used these two rocks for. The round one is an inch thick and of solid black rock, and the other one is oblong and exactly a half inch through, and of perfectly white rock."

The girls called him again, and he hobbled to the door with me, saying, "Be sure and go by the gin and ask the boys to show you how it is operated."

• • •

When I reached the McLeroy Brothers Gin the next morning there was a middle-aged man sitting on a split-bottom chair leaning against the building, holding the reins of the mules standing in front of the mill, while their master was unloading corn to be ground into meal. I asked the man if he was Mr. McLeroy's brother.

"No, ma'am, I am just their first cousin, but I hang around here when I don't have nothing else to do. You will find them inside. Just go on in."

The man who was standing at the grinder, grinding meal when

I entered the building didn't see me at first. Finally he looked up and came toward me.

"Good morning. What can I do for you?"

I explained my visit to him. He nodded his head, pointed his thumb over his shoulder, and said in a gruff voice, "Go in the gin house. You will find my brother in there mending a belt. He will tell you what you want to know. I haven't got time myself. I have fifty bushels of corn to grind into meal right away."

I followed his directions and found his brother mending the belt. After I had explained what I wanted, he said, "I never was a hand to explain things so a person could understand what I'm talking about, but I'll be glad to show you around and tell you what I know about it.

"My father turned this over to us five boys about twenty years ago. If you like this kind of work, it is very interesting. There used to be money in this sort of work when we took it over. All of us have families and from the proceeds of this we have done the best we could by them, educated our children and have given them a few advantages of life.

"I've seen the time when we ginned cotton day and night, of course in season. And we have ginned as high as thirty-three hundred bales of cotton in one season. Times were good then, but since that time there has come an awful change. Each year we have ginned less and less cotton. Last year was our shortest year and we only ginned six hundred and thirty bales. As a rule, a man can pay for his ginning out of his seed from the cotton. It cost around $2.50 to gin a bale, but this year, as I see it now, the seed from a bale won't pay for it; as cotton seed is selling for seventy-five cents a hundred pounds.

"Do you see that pipe that begins over there by the door? The cotton is hauled here and the people drive on those scales in front of the door. After the cotton is weighed, that suction pipe is placed in the wagon of cotton and draws the cotton into the gin. This wheel here is governed by air control and when that large pipe is full it trips the wheel. The air is cut off until the pipe is cleared and it cuts on again."

He opened the drums, explaining, "This is where the seed is taken from the cotton. The brushes back of the saw cut and card the cotton as it is cut from the seed by the saws in front of the brush. These seeds go through the trough until they reach the trap door here. Do you see this roller? Well, it turns the seed into the pipe below and they are carried through that pipe until they reach the seed house at the corner of the lot cut there.

"While that is going on, the cotton drops in this hopper. When it is full, do you see this round circle in the floor? We spring the trap and this round section revolves to where the bale is shaped. Where the bagging and ties are placed, as this hopper fills with cotton to be pressed into bales, it gradually rises until the bottom of the bale reaches the level of the floor.

"Then the ties are buckled over the bagging that holds the cotton.

"These stalls are used for storing seed. Do you see those trap doors at the back of the stalls near the floor? They open into a suction pipe. Often we store the seed for a man, and he will decide to sell us the seed. After the purchase is made, we open those doors and the seed is carried to the seed house through a pipe. Lots of times a man will haul cotton here in the rain, and the cotton is stored in those stalls until it is dry enough to gin.

"We don't make no extra charge for those things, for a fellow in business has to do lots of accommodating to hold his customers.

"During ginning season we work night and day. It keeps all of us on the jump, and we hire quite a lot of help. Some we pay two dollars a day and others three dollars.

"Of course we do pay a few as low as seventy-five cents. Three dollars a day includes day and night work. I couldn't say how much we make, as what we make is divided among us boys, and we at least make enough to keep our families from starving.

"Fifteen or say eighteen years ago, however, we made a good living out of ginning and gave our children a few advantages and a college education. So far, our children don't have to help us, but we are getting old now, and if the ginning business keeps dropping off, there is no telling what they will have to do.

"Since this country has cut down on cotton acreage, other countries are doubling theirs. Take Australia, which at one time was considered a small cotton country. It doubled its acreage in the last two years. Instead of this country exporting our cotton and cotton goods to other countries raising cotton, they are importing it to us each year by the million bales of both cotton and cloth.

"But I'm sure the reduction of acreage in this country is all right in its way, and those in charge surely know better than we what it is all about.

"Now come this way, and I'll show you the grist mill. All this machinery in here controls it. This is the corn sifter. After the corn is shelled it is put in the sifter. This sifter has a fan under it that blows the cornsilk from the corn, and the sifter catches the large pieces of cobs.

"The corn is then taken through the overhead pipe controlled by those belts you see, and is spilled into a smaller sifter where every particle of dust, dirt, and small bits of cobs are either blown out or left in the sifter. It then goes to the grinder and comes out nice clean meal. You won't find any worms, weevils, and trash in our meal.

"Some people just grind all that up in the meal, but we try to be careful about ours. We used to grind lots of meal, but now we grind just whatever amount of corn is brought to us.

"Look out of the window, and you'll see our mill for chopping oats up into foodstuff stock. It is over to the left. That small contraption to the right is where we saw shingles. We take the lumber and saw it into the desired length, them feed it to the machine, and, as you know, one end of the shingle is much thicker than the other. Since composition and tin roofs are used now, we have very few calls for our shingles.

"The sacks you see back of you here in the building are full of meal and corn. You are right, this machinery is dangerous, and you have to be on your guard at all times. But so far, none of us McLeroys have been hurt in the past twenty years, but we did have a Negro to get his hand cut off in the cotton gin, and another his arm."

While we were talking, a woman dressed in a pink crepe dress and a boy in overalls drove up in front, with two mules hitched to a wagon. The woman and boy were sitting on a board laid across the front of the wagon. There were several sacks of corn, chickens, eggs, and watermelons in the back. The woman had her straight hair tucked back of her ears. She spat a mouthful of tobacco on the ground, addressing Mr. McLeroy.

"Do you have time to grind this corn by twelve o'clock?"

"Yes, I think so."

"All right," said the woman. "Git out of this here wagon, boy, and yank them there sacks of corn out. You know I've got to git to town and sell my chicken and watermelons before folks beat me selling theirs."

"God Helped Us"

Editor's Note: Mrs. Ina B. Hawkes interviewed Mrs. Luther Crawford on Aug. 28, 1939, and the interview was edited by John N. Booth, of the Augusta, Georgia WPA office. In the 1942 Athens City Directory, a Luther P. Crawford is listed as being married to Willie Crawford, who we presume to be the Mrs. Luther Crawford interviewed in 1939. Mr. Crawford was a long-time member of the Clarke County School Board. The Crawfords lived on the Danielsville Road on Rural Route #2.

In the 1947 city directory, Mr. Crawford is listed by himself, possibly indicating that his wife had died. I have not found any information about the Crawfords' death dates. They may have moved from Clarke County to other Georgia or non-Georgia locations.

• • •

"Yes, we live right across the road here," said Mr. Crawford.

"Oh, yes, it's my wife you want to see. I'm sure she'll talk to you, because she likes company. Just go on up there and I'll be there to let you in just as soon as I can put this school bus under shelter."

Approaching the modern frame house, I admired the shrubbery that enhanced the appearance of the well-kept place. I had to go around to the back door where Mr. Crawford met me and assisted me up the steps into a tidy kitchen.

Coming in out of the glare of the afternoon sun, I didn't see anyone at first, but when my eyes were accustomed to the shadows, I saw a woman sitting very still in a corner of the room. Her face was illuminated by a bright smile.

"I've brought you some company," said Mr. Crawford, when he had introduced me to his wife.

"Sit down over here by me," she said, as I repeated my name to her. "I was just ironing some pants for my husband, but it's not necessary that I finish them now."

It seemed incredible that a person so drawn and twisted in body should be able to iron clothing, especially difficult pieces such as men's trousers.

"Did you really iron those pants?" I inquired.

"Oh, yes," she proudly answered. "I ironed them, and I do all my work now, but I guess I'd better tell you something about my earlier life and about how I got like this.

"My life at home as a girl I won't say much about. I went to school in Danielsville, Georgia, and then I taught for fifteen years in three different schools. Believe it or not, in teaching all three schools I never went but five miles from home. I always went on horseback; you see, we were country people. My father always said, 'If you can teach at home, what's the use of going abroad?'

"My sister had typhoid fever, and it went into rheumatism, which left her crippled for life. It fell to my lot to wait on her. I taught school in the spring and summer. After my long hours at school, I'd start nursing her soon as I returned home. You see, she was in such a fix she couldn't stand the covers or nightgowns to touch her. I finally had to quit teaching. I just went to bed with her, night and day, to hold the covers so they wouldn't press on her anywhere.

"Now, you can imagine what a strain I was in. This went on for weeks. When the doctor came one day and found us like that, he flew into a rage and said, 'This has to be stopped! There's no use in both girls dying.'

"My mother was not well, either, at that time. I'd met Mr. Crawford here—I still call him Mr. Crawford—and we were planning to get married, but it looked as though I couldn't leave home, with no one to look after my mother and sister.

"You see, I always felt that way about them. I wasn't sure either what married life would be like; that kept me back some.

"After my sister died, my married brother and his wife said they'd take care of mother. Mr. Crawford and I married after I was thirty-three years old. My father had left me a small sum of money, and we decided the best thing to do was invest it in land.

"The year after our marriage—in 1912—our baby was born dead. Somehow I could never blame the doctors, for I had the best of care, but it left me helpless. I haven't walked a step in long over twenty years now.

"No, I don't use crutches or a wheel chair either. You can see why I am like this today.

"Well, things were going fairly well with our crop. Mr. Crawford had to take care of me, for no one could do me any good but him. He worked with me night and day and for four years continuously, getting up sometimes twenty-five or thirty times a night, and sometimes not even going to bed a-tall.

"It went on like that until he became so exhausted that he would completely give out and fall asleep. Sometimes it would be impossible for me to wake him. You see, I suffered agonies all over, and when he went to sleep, I couldn't 'rouse him a-tall.

"He decided to pull my cot up to his bed at night—we didn't sleep together then—and tie a string around my finger and then tie it to his hand. Then, when I couldn't stand it another minute, I'd pull the string. I'd have to keep on pulling harder and harder sometimes, for he'd be so tired and worn out that when I pulled the string he'd just shake it off his hand, and turn over and go to sleep.

"Well, he gave me a stick to punch him with, but I was so weak and gradually losing use of myself, till I couldn't use the stick to any advantage. He kept on working with me and having me treated until finally I got to combing my hair, and then I found I could use my limbs a little.

"It was a terrible sorrow to me when I began to lose strength again, and for twelve months I lay helpless again. One night during this relapse our home caught fire. When they came to get me out of the house, it took four men to hold me. I was carried to that little cabin you see out there in the back yard.

"I was still suffering bad, but the doctor said he couldn't give me much dope. He was afraid I'd get in the habit of taking it. I'm telling you this because I was determined not to be a dope addict.

"The doctor advised Mr. Crawford to give me some whiskey, but that didn't ease my pains.

"Mr. Crawford and I decided that we were not living up to God's word and will as we should. Now this is where my life changed. I'd always been a Presbyterian, but a lady came and talked to me one day about my soul, and she told me about Christian Science.

The doctors weren't doing me any good, so the lady taught Mr. Crawford and me to declare and affirm the truth. After we had kept this up a long time, I began to move my head and arms. Soon I was stronger. I only weighed seventy-eight pounds when I put my whole heart and mind on God. You see, until we understand and stay steadfast with God we don't get any relief from Him. We cling to Him; we know He is divine love. He has done so much for me since I learned to declare and affirm His love and promises.

"We lived in that cabin in the yard for twelve years. Mr. Crawford continued to plant crops of cotton, corn, and vegetables. Of course, we still had our land. We even saved a little money, and with a loan we built this house we are living in now.

"With God's help, Mr. Crawford takes me up every morning, dresses me, and puts me in this chair where I'm sitting now. With the help of this chair I can go most any place I want to. He made it just for me. It's the only one I can get about in.

"In the mornings, we first come to the kitchen for breakfast. Here, I'll show you how I walk in my chair."

To demonstrate, she folded her gnarled arms as best she could and placed her toes on the floor, then reared back and twisted about one way and then the other, forcing the chair, which was a little higher than the ordinary straight chair, across the floor. She propelled it with almost incredible speed.

"I carry my chair with me to church and everywhere else that I have to get out of the car," she said. "After we get to the kitchen, I fix the table and other little things about breakfast while Mr. Crawford makes the biscuits. I can't use my fingers enough to make them.

"After breakfast, I wash dishes, churn, sweep the floor, and I even do our washing and, well, you caught me ironing. The reason I'm using this coal-heating sad iron is because my electric iron is being fixed. I burned it out the other day."

I had been so interested in Mrs. Crawford's talk that I hadn't realized it was beginning to grow dark. I suddenly knew that I had to go, but first I asked her permission to look through the house.

"I was wanting you to," she replied. "I want you to see my rock mantel. Mr. Crawford and I value it so much."

The mantel, beautifully designed and finished, was in the dining room. The furniture here was plain, but clean and well kept. In the bedroom everything was arranged so that Mrs. Crawford could do her own house work. Noticing that she had only one narrow cot in the room, I asked where Mr. Crawford slept.

She laughed, "That's all we need. I'd have twin beds or a double bed, but you see, I have to have Mr. Crawford to brace me at night, and he might roll away from me in a double bed.

"I can go to bed now and sleep like a baby because I work all day. I never hire any work done. Sometimes people come along wanting something to eat or wear and I let 'em help me out some then so they can earn what they need so bad."

"Do you own your house now, Mrs. Crawford? You said something about a loan or mortgage on it," I inquired.

"Well, we're still paying on it, and if we keep loving God, we'll soon get it paid for. That's where God helped us again. You see, the mortgage was to be paid off on a certain day. We'd put in for another loan and it hadn't gone through, so of course the place was advertised for sale. Well, the man that put the house up didn't show up at the sale a-tall, and in a few days the loan went through and we used it to pay off the old mortgage.

"We've managed to make our payments on the new loan regularly ever since.

"I have my telephone fixed so I can carry it anywhere over the house that I want to. When I go to any part of the house I always take it with me. I have friends that I've never seen that call me 'most every day for a chat.

"I take orders over the telephone for our farm produce and have it sent in to town 'most every day. And, too, I have my electric lights, Frigidaire, electric iron, and radio.

"Most of all I have my God, who is the cause of my having what I have today.

"I do lots of political work on my telephone, too. You see, that's the only way that I can help, and I do all I can that way."

As I prepared to leave, I told her, "I've enjoyed this short visit with you, Mrs. Crawford."

"I'm so glad you came, and do come again or call me sometimes over the telephone," she said, as she walked her chair toward the front door.

Principal of Grammar School
Thirty-Three Years
ᘇ❧♣❧ᘊ

Editor's Note: Mrs. Mary Wright Hill was interviewed on July 27, 1939, by Mrs. Sadie B. Hornsby. Mrs. Hill, a pioneer Athens black educator, was living at 525 W. Hancock Avenue. The house is still in good condition in 2001. She was listed as principal of the East Athens School in the 1938 city directory. She was married to Squire W. Hill, who had a drapery business. She been married earlier to George H. Reid and to John H. Deadwyler.

Mrs. Hill's will was probated in the December, 1946, court term, in Athens. Her husband was given the use of their home for his lifetime, and one of Mrs. Hill's daughters, Vivian Reid Beavers, was to inherit it upon his death. Another daughter, Marinita Reid Young, was to receive a house at 269 Finley St.

• • •

"Do have a chair," said Mary Wright Hill. "They don't look so comfortable, but they are. I'm proud of them, even if they are old and out of date. My daughter wants me to sell them, but I don't intend to as long as I live because they were sent to me from Africa as a wedding gift.

"Bishop Harrison of Atlanta was stationed there, and as he was a good friend of our family, I sent him an invitation to my wedding. These are what I got from him for a wedding gift. You'll have to excuse me a minute. I picked a gallon of figs from my own bush this morning and had just put them on the stove to make preserves; they'll burn if I don't cut the electric current from under them."

Mary Wright Hill is of medium height and weight. Her curly black hair is streaked with gray and is cut very short in the back, which causes it to bush out around her face. She wears glasses and has piercing brown eyes.

She was wearing a blue print dress buttoned down the back, black slippers and tan hose. Her dress was none too clean, and the hose were spotted and soiled. I thought the large smudge of soot on her arm was a birthmark until she took the hem of her dress and tried to wipe it off. The contents of the room were very old but well arranged, and the general appearance showed the use of a broom had long been neglected.

She soon returned, saying to me, "I will have to talk briefly because this is my husband's busy day and I have to help him. He is an interior decorator and has a large order of shades to put up at the Co-ordinate College. I went with him out to Winterville last night to hang curtains he made for a lady.

"No, ma'am, I don't know what he makes, for we have never asked each other that question, because he has his profession and I have mine. He makes a living all right and says he has never been without a day's work in his life. He works hard and saves some for a rainy day.

"No, I wasn't borned in Athens. I came here to teach. My mother and father were born in Greenville, North Carolina. After they married, they moved to Asheville, and there is where I was born on March 6, 1881. As you can see, I am more Indian and French than Negro. My grandmother was a Negro and my grandfather was an Indian. On my grandfather's side his mother was a Negro and his father a Frenchman.

"When Atlanta was on a building boom, he moved his family there, where he could get plenty of work to do. He was a contractor for brick work. He made plenty of money, bought a home there, and educated the three oldest children.

"There were six of we children, all educated from Atlanta University, but one who graduated at Tuskegee under Booker T. Washington. He [that child] took up the same trade as my father.

"My father died when I was seven years of age. Before I finished high school, my mother became an invalid, and before I finished Atlanta University she lost her eyesight. My desire was to become a medical doctor. Not having funds and no one to help me, I chose teaching to help my mother and educate the younger children.

"My older brother and sisters helped my mother and sent me to college, but I paid most of my own way working at school while I was there.

"After I had to quit school I was given a place teaching at Oxford, Georgia, at the age of thirteen. There were two grown people teaching under me. I was paid thirty dollars a month. With that amount, my living came out of it and the rest was sent home to my mother. After teaching at Oxford two years I accepted work in Athens. I taught school out here in a section called Brooklyn.

"I taught at Brooklyn school two years, making thirty-five dollars a month. At the end of that time I was elected principal of East Athens School. I am now serving there and have been there thirty-three years this past January.

"I was the first colored woman to be elected principal in Athens. There was a woman appointed to fill an unexpired term, but I was the first woman elected to serve. I filled the vacancy of the principal, who accepted a position in Panama for one hundred dollars, and he only made forty dollars here.

"When I first took the place as principal, the school was just a four-room wooden building with no modern conveniences. The

Mary Wright Hill's home at 525 W. Hancock Ave. Taken in 2001.
Photo credit: Al Hester

toilets were just topsoil privies, and we got our drinking water from wells. The enrollment was around 190 children for the five grades, and three teachers. The school has grown to a ten-room building, has sanitary toilets, running water, electric lights, and a telephone. The enrollment used to run as high as 600; now we have around 450 pupils and eight teachers.

"One reason our attendance has decreased in that section, is lots of the Negroes have moved North in order to find work, as there is not enough work here for everybody, and people are not able to pay a high price for colored help.

"I would like to tell you how I managed to get running water in that school. Not long after I took charge and began to drink that well water, I began to feel bad and didn't feel like doing my work as it should be done.

"No matter how hard I talked to the city officials, they

wouldn't do anything about it. I took drinking water from home and began to work on the State Board of Health about the conditions of the water in the section. They sent a representative down to investigate the matter.

"They asked me a million questions, which they had a perfect right to do. I sent a boy to the well to get a fresh bucket of water and saw to it that the bottle I put the sample in was thoroughly clean. They took it and went on back to Atlanta. In about a month I got a report on that water.

"Headquarters said they didn't understand why there wasn't typhoid fever and other contagious diseases over there. Water was put in and not long after that the Health Department here employed a young lady to examine all those things as they were brought to the attention of the department, and specimens were brought in to be examined.

"I have done everything over there but marry a couple and embalm a body, because of financial conditions which existed in that service.

"I used to teach the fifth grade. That wouldn't work, because the children who reached me I found didn't have a good foundation in the beginning.

"For it's like this—the first grade is where the children get their foundation for the fundamentals of school work. If they are started wrong, they will have a time for the rest of their lives.

"The things I have seen over there would make you sick. Often I have had a kid come to school sick. Their parents [have been] at work, and I have put a pallet on the floor by the heater many days and laid a sick child on it, given them milk and food, and have taken that child home or to some friend's house until the mother came home late in the afternoon.

"When I first started teaching in the school, I wore my good clothes. I have looked down on my dress and seen lice crawling on it, or have a sick child to vomit, or have a bowel action and get it on me. I decided to wear white dresses in order to see the lice when they fell on my white dress.

"I have had people ask me, 'Why do you wear white dresses to school the year 'round? Are you a nurse?' I would give them some nice answer and go on.

"I found it was necessary to know something about nursing and the care of children, not only my own, but those I taught. So I took a course by mail and received my diploma from the Chatauqua School of Nursing, at Jamestown, New York. That course has been my salvation in caring for those children.

Now when things like I have just mentioned occur, I immediately get the mercurochrome and wet their heads in it. It kills every nit and louse on a child's head.

"The school is in a Baptist area. I had an awful time when I first went over there. The first exercise was a perfect flop, as those people are on the order of Primitive Baptist. If the children had to skip or take a few steps that looked like dancing, their mother would take 'em out.

"Now they are educated to know all those things help a child to have grace and poise, as well as to help them overcome their timidity to perform before a crowd.

"Oh, I always have enemies and there are plenty of men and women who would stoop to do anything to get my job. The superintendent called me in his office one day. I couldn't imagine what he wanted.

"He said, 'Mary, I want to talk to you about your work, for you may have heard there are some of your race trying to get your place, but I don't want you to worry about it, so long as you are doing as fine work as you are now. Two men came in my office the other day and one of them said to me, "I understand you have an opening." "An opening for what?" I asked. "Well," I told him, "I don't have an opening for a man, and I won't have one for you soon."'

"I thanked the superintendent and left his office. That shows you how people will do you behind your back.

"I started in at forty dollars a mouth, but I have made $135. We teachers have been cut, so I am ashamed to tell anybody what I make now. Aside from being the first woman principal, I was the first Negro woman to volunteer in this section to teach the illiterate adults, to raise Georgia in the seals[sic] of illiteracy, because she was way down.

"This adult school operated ten years and the board paid twenty-five a month for nine years. I gave my services free the first year. We had an enrollment of over one hundred Negroes who could neither read nor write. The classes were held two nights a week, Tuesday and Thursday, from eight until ten o'clock.

"The school closed because the Board of Education did not have money enough to pay the teachers.

"Also I have taught social service work for ten years. A representative from Washington, D. C., came down to thank me for my work. There was a contest put on in three large cities and [in] some way Athens pulled strings and got it for the one small town to compete, with all the schools here doing outstanding child health demonstration work.

"When I put on that demonstration and wrote my thesis I had a dream I would be the winner. When I was notified I had won the trophy, I couldn't believe my ears. And the funniest thing about it was the superintendent of our city schools didn't want me to take it home with me.

"His secretary said, 'Why, it doesn't belong to the city. It was given to the individual winning it. So by rights it belongs to Mary and we have no right to keep it.'

"Very reluctantly he presented the cup to me, saying, 'You should have civic pride enough to put it on display where everyone could see it.'

"I told him I surely had that and asked one of the jewelers to place it in their display windows for me. The jeweler did and insisted that I should let him polish it for me, but I liked it dull best.

"Before I came to Athens to teach, my mother called me to her, saying, 'Daughter, there is something I want you to do. You know my days are numbered, and after I am gone, there will be nobody to educate my younger children but you, so just as soon as you find a good man I want you to marry and make a home for yourself and the children, and educate them.'

"But, Mama," I said, "Why don't you tell Dora that? She is older than I and, too, I want to study and become a medical doctor." She pleaded with me and finally I told her I would.

"Soon after I came here to teach I met my first husband. We decided to marry. I had said I was going to have a church wedding, and it took me two years to buy my clothes, as I had to send a certain part of my salary to my mother, as my sister was at Atlanta University and my brother was attending Tuskegee.

"My wedding dress and veil was beautiful, and I paid a modiste who was well known in Atlanta $12.50 to make my wedding gown. I paid for every detail myself connected with the wedding except my bouquet, the flowers for the bridesmaids, and boutonnieres for the groomsmen.

"We were married on Christmas Day. One year from that day my oldest child was born, and eighteen months later another little girl. She was born on the Fourth of July.

"I just have the two girls. My oldest girl was four-and-a-half years old when my husband died. We had just bought this home and he had just made one payment. I was determined not to lose it, and I set out to work harder than ever.

"I have taught all day and nursed at night. In the summer I closed my house, paid one of my sisters to keep my girls, and nursed the summer through.

"The girls went to the same school where I am principal. After they finished grammar school, they went to high school. After finishing there, I sent my oldest girl to Fisk University, and the other one finished Atlanta University. My oldest daughter got her degree at Fisk University majoring in history. After she left Fisk she taught in Springfield College in Springfield, Mass.

"Her most outstanding work was done as social worker at that college. She was selected one of the two colored girls in America to travel in Europe with a group of white students to study students in other countries. She visited Italy, Germany, Austria, Hungary, France, Switzerland, and England.

"While in England a lady took a fancy to her and presented her with a lovely ring. It surely made the other students jealous. Now you need not mention this, for if you do, the Negroes will say if they know I told you, 'Old Lady Hill is bragging.'

"Negroes are just like magpies, always jabbering about what people are proud of. You bet I am, for I worked hard for my children and they have done well.

"The first time my daughter was offered that trip to Europe she couldn't accept it, as we didn't have the money, but she told them she would be ready the next time that trip was offered to her. That trip cost us $2,000.

"The head of the social work in New York sent a representative down to see if Viola had everything she needed. She went all through her clothes, checked her linen, and the only thing she didn't have was an air cushion to sit on while traveling in Europe. You know all the trains have wooden seats. I couldn't find one in Athens.

"Viola went to Atlanta and paid six dollars for that cushion. When she returned from abroad, she told me that six dollars was well spent.

"That social worker told me while she was here, she had no

idea Negroes in the South knew what such environment was or that they had such nice homes. We took her back to the hotel in our car.

"Don't misunderstand me, I am a Southern Negro and know my place. Therefore we treated her as we knew and were taught to act around white people. When she invited us to her room to have tea, we refused, knowing the excitement it would create following a white woman into a hotel to have tea.

"My other daughter didn't apply herself, so she didn't do as well as the one I have just told you about. She got a job in New York as social worker. She met and married a musician.

"Nanette made good money, so her husband gave up his orchestra and sat down on her to support him. She had to stop work after her second child came. She lost her job and couldn't find work.

"After divorcing her husband, she got a job with the WPA as a social worker and now is getting on all right.

"Viola married an Atlanta man. She has a little girl of her own and don't work any more. I often tell her she ought to do something after all the money she and I have spent on her education. However, I am proud of the man she married and hope they will make a go of it. I gave both of my girls church weddings, and as I have told you about my race, you have never heard of such a to-do as they did make over the girls' church weddings, and every one I heard that had anything ugly to say about it we excluded them from among our invited guests.

"I stayed single fourteen years before I married again, because I didn't want any other man having a say-so over my children. When I did marry after the girls were grown and out on their own, the man was an overgrown, spoiled man. His people had money, and he thought because I had a nice home and a good job he would let me take care of him.

"I gave him all the chance in the world to get out and hunt work. Still he wouldn't do it. So one day I said to him, 'Look here, haven't you found any work yet?'

"After I learned he hadn't tried, I told him it was time to get going. He thought I didn't mean it at first. When I let him know I meant what I said, he went back to his mother.

"About a month later she brought him back to me and begged me to take him back. I asked him if he had a job, and he told me he thought so. 'Well,' I told him, 'you didn't bring anything with you, but yourself and a few clothes in a trunk, and you haven't bought one thing since you have been here. Now get your belongings and get out for good. This time I mean for you to stay out.'

"About three years ago I married my present husband, after I had got my divorce from my second husband. He is a good man and hard working. We work together and save our money so when we get too old to work we will have something to live on. He is getting old. He will be sixty-nine his next birthday and I do all I can to help him.

"I drive him where he has to go in my car. That saves him lots of steps. He is good to me and I try to be to him. He owns his own property but has it rented out. I didn't want to live in his house, so he stored his furniture and I am much happier where I have always lived.

"Many are the nights I have stayed awake crying when my children were asleep, wondering what I would do next and how to meet my bills, but I always found a way. Now I don't owe any money, and I rent another house I have built on the back of my lot. This was a large lot, and I have often thought about that wasted space. So when I got this one paid for, I bought lumber and had a nice four-room house built, and rent from it paid for the lumber.

"This house I live in has ten rooms. Come on and let us show it to you. I am proud of it because it represents many a hard day's work and worry."

I followed her into a bedroom. She continued to talk.

"You can see how old my furniture is. Why, every piece in this room is at least thirty years old. You will have to excuse the dirt and dust, as we just came back Monday from a visit to my husband's daughters in Ohio."

She laughed and said, "They wanted to see what their new step-mother looked like, so they sent us the money to go on. After visiting them for two weeks, we went to see my people in Chicago, then on to New York to visit my daughter. While there we took in the World's Fair.

"Come in here. I call this small room a den. I fixed this up for my husband so when his customers come he can work out their plans without being bothered."

In the room was a studio couch with many bright cushions on it, Morris chair, desk, bookcase, a table with an electric lamp on it. On the floor was a gay-colored wool rug, while at the short windows were pink curtains and red drapes. She picked up a small notebook from the arm of the Morris chair, saying, "Well, bless my time, here is the book my husband has been looking for ever since he came back from our trip. This book he keeps his orders in and the style of curtains and draperies he draws for the customers. He will be lost without it, as he has several orders to fill right away.

"Now, come, let me show you the kitchen. You see I have all modern equipment, as we are not able to hire our work done. Our electric stove and refrigerator are a perfect joy.

"As you can see, all the furniture in my dining room is real old. Look at that fruit basket of Dresden china. Aren't those colors delicate and pretty? In this china cabinet I have several very old pieces of hand-painted china. I want you to look at that tureen on the buffet. I never saw one like it before, and I have never used it for fear of breaking it.

"The lamp on my dining table was a gift from a young man in California, in appreciation for what I did for his mother. I took my daughters out to Los Angeles on a visit to some school friends of mine. While I was there the woman next door was taken violently ill. We ran over to see what we could do for her. I administered first aid until the doctor arrived to keep her alive.

"When he arrived, we both worked like wildfire to save her, but nothing revived her. She died three hours later with her head on my arm. Our time was up for us to leave to visit other places in that state. Before leaving I did all I could about the funeral arrangements before her only child could get there from Denver.

"After visiting several cities, we arrived home. Three weeks later I found a huge box at my front door, and when I unpacked it this is what I found.

"This bust of an Indian woman I bought while in Chicago. My girls laughed at me, but I didn't care. The only interest I had in it is because my mother was the image of that bust in her last days. I told you in the beginning I am more Indian and French than Negro. We are descendants of the Cherokee Indians, and my mother was only one-eighth Negro.

"The corner of the bust got broken some way, but I wouldn't take the world for it.

"I want you to see the room I pride more than any of the others in the house, because every piece of the furniture in my living room was a wedding gift from my first husband, and other odds and ends are from close friends. A furniture store here offered me seventy-five dollars for this suite, but I told him that was my price for the chairs only.

"Of course, the radio, piano, and that end table my trophy sits on are modern, but I have had them at least twenty years. Do you see those two large pictures of child subjects on the wall? One of my daughters told me they were so old-fashioned and out-of-date, why didn't I take them to the back room. I told her they suited me, and I meant to keep them where I could see them as long as I lived, for they represented the first money I ever made when I was eight years old.

"I kept a colored woman's children for her while she worked out for white people. She paid me $1.50 a week. I gave $1.00 of it to my mother and put 50 cents of it on the pictures. They cost $2.50 each, and I paid on them each week until I finished paying for them.

"No, ma'am, I never worked for white people. Therefore, I missed my only chance of ever going to Europe. There was a very wealthy white man in Atlanta whose daughter married. He begged me to go with her as her maid to Europe, as he wanted an educated person who was old enough to advise her. Not having worked for white people, I was afraid I wouldn't fill my place efficiently at that age, so they sent to Washington and got a maid who was educated and had some knowledge of nursing.

"Come in the hall. I want to show you a picture of my mother that was taken after she went blind. I paid a photographer twenty-five dollars to make that picture for me. One of my white friends who was a teacher—she is dead now—had a larger picture of the Madonna to fall from the wall in her room, and the corner was broken off the frame, and there were large dirty places on the canvas. The school wanted to have it repaired for her, but she told them, 'No, give it to Mary for her school. She will know just what to do with it.'

"I took some brown wax crayon, went over the soiled places, and put each tiny piece of the broken frame back in place. It is now in my assembly room, and you can't even tell where the damaged part was.

"Every one of my friends know how I love pictures. That is why that lady gave me her broken picture.

"I want to show you upstairs. When the girls began to get large enough to have a room of their own, I had the roof of the house raised and added these bedrooms, bath, and sleeping porch. It is awfully hot up here. I don't use it now—only when the girls come home on a visit.

"After I went to all this expense, my girls left home. This front room is Viola's. If you notice, I have furnished the room in the color suited to her name in curtains at the window, scarves and bedspread, and scatter rugs. You can see the furniture is cheap, but good enough for us.

"This is my youngest daughter's room. It is done in pink. Anything I did for her was all right, so that's why she had an iron bed and the other bed is wooden.

"Both rooms are just like they left them. This large room isn't as nice, so when they had company the girls slept in here with me. As you can see, the furniture in this room is odds and ends of very old furniture.

"The coolest room up here is the sleeping porch."

I followed her down the steps, through a curtain, and entered a small hall. The door in front of me opened into the bathroom.

Mary said, "I had this old wardrobe fitted in this space of the hall to hold my linens."

She opened the double doors, and every shelf was filled with various household linens, put on the shelves at random.

"This is the sleeping porch," she said, opening the door that leads into the room. There was a white iron bed with a candlewick spread on it, large dark oak dresser, and table with with a reading lamp on it.

Mary said, "I am ashamed for you to see this room, everything so torn up. Clothes everywhere, but I did want you to see this old desk. My first husband was a barber and was employed by a German, who, when he went out of business, gave it to my husband as a gift of appreciation for his faithful work.

"The man brought it to America from Germany when he came over. Let's go downstairs. I want to show you the goldfish pool. I made it myself with the help of a young boy I paid fifty cents."

When we reached the porch, she said, "Come this way to the terrace. Here is my pool. The water lilies haven't done so well this year. On real hot nights I come out here and sit in the pergola. I am proud of my house because I bought and paid for it myself, which represents several thousand dollars.

"I get ten dollars a month for the one you see back of my house. Lots of Negroes will spend everything they make on their back, things to eat, and a car, but I try to even mine up, and I didn't buy my Dodge until I felt I could afford it.

"When my children were small, and up the street nearer town, nothing but Jews lived along there. They used to tell me, 'Mary, your children are going to be bowlegged, you walk them so far back and forth to school. Why don't you take a streetcar?'

"'Because I can't afford it,' I would tell them. 'That thirty cents a day would buy food for us.'

"They stayed well, for I learned in my course the proper food to give them and how to prepare it. Therefore, I have been fortunate when it came to doctor bills.

"I contribute [sic] my success to hard work, saving, and praying. I joined the church when I was eleven years of age, and am a member of the First Congregational Church of Atlanta, Georgia, and I promised the Lord if he would help me I would live a good Christian life and teach others the way they should live.

"When my children came and were old enough to understand, I did my best to instill in them the way they should live. They have never disappointed me, and as a whole I am very proud of my family, for as far as I have been able to learn, generations back, all my people have been good Christian men and women.

"Yes, ma'am. I mean to teach as long as the Board of Education will let me. I put all there is in me in my work. Many a teacher goes to school and teaches enough to get by on. That isn't the way I do. While I am not teaching I am thinking of the children next fall, planning my work, things that are best for the children.

"So many children go to school without a scrap of paper or a pencil. During the summer I save every piece of paper that is useable and every pencil I find. Lots of times I find one in the street, and I pick it up even if they are not more than one or two inches long.

"Now next fall when school opens, when a child don't have pencil or paper, there will be plenty for those who need it."

Her husband came to the door and called his wife.

"Baby, I am ready to go hang those shades now. Miss, if you hear of anybody who wants interior decorating done, I would appreciate it if you would tell them about me."

After thanking Mary for the story and telling her husband I would keep his work in mind, I left them scurrying toward the car with an armful of shades.

Mrs. Janie Bradberry Harris, WPA Project Supervisor

Editor's Note: Mrs. Janie Bradberry Harris was a widow, interviewed by Mrs. Sadie B. Hornsby on Feb. 25, 1939. Mrs. Harris lived on Tallassee Road, Rural Route #2. In the 1938 Athens City Directory she was listed as a seamstress, working for the WPA, with her name given as "Jennie" instead of Janie. As she indicates, she held several different jobs with the local WPA office. Information concerning her birth or death dates has not been found.

• • •

Mrs. Harris was sitting at her desk, busy making out reports.

"Are you too busy to talk to me this morning?" I asked her.

"It all depends on what it is and how long it will take you. You know I can't take my working hours to talk personal matters," she said. "But first tell me what it is you want to know?"

I told Mrs. Harris I would like to get her life history and wanted one of a WPA Project Supervisor.

"What do you want me to tell you?"

I asked her if I could see her at her home. "Why, yes if you have a way to get out to my house, but I live 'way out on Tallassee Road. I guess I can talk and work, too. I am waiting for my head boss to come, and since I am not so busy this rainy day, I expect you had better see me now."

Mrs. Harris is a large woman weighing about 200 pounds. She has gray hair and wears glasses. She was wearing a one-piece black dress; the skirt and sleeves were crepe and the body of the waist was cut velvet. She also wore black slippers and gray hose. She seemed very much interested in her work.

She began, "I was raised right here in Clarke County and was the oldest of seven. There were three girls and four boys in our family. There is nothing interesting about my childhood. We played and scrapped as children will do, and when we were large enough, we helped in the field if there was anything for us to do.

"I dropped corn and beans many a day and picked cotton. I was a good cotton picker. I remember distinctly there is a big difference back when I was a child and now.

"My father was an overseer for a man who had a large farm. We had plenty to eat and wear. We raised everything we ate at home. My father was also a basket weaver and made some of the daintiest little baskets you ever saw. He sold lots of them, but most of his income was from selling cattle—he raised lots of them for sale.

"When my sister and I wanted a new hat or dress, we sold eggs, milk, butter, apples or anything else we could find to sell. We lived near Barnett Shoals, and we could always dispose of any surplus supplies we couldn't use, selling things to the people who worked in the mill.

"I remember I had a cousin who worked in the cotton mill at Barnett Shoals. Whenever I went to see her, she would save up all the tin buckets and give them to me to take home. We thought we were rich when we got them tin buckets—they were rare things for country people to have.

"When I was fourteen years old, I bought a sewing machine. I ordered it from Sears and Roebuck, and paid for it sewing for Negroes.

"When they were building the electric plant at Barnett Shoals, my sister and I used to sell buttermilk to the men working on the plant for five cents a glass. My favorite sport was horse-back riding, believe it or not. You wouldn't think it true to look at me now.

"We attended Sunday school in a country school house, the same building we went to school in. All my people are Baptist. I was fourteen years old when I joined church at Corinth Baptist Church and was baptized in Big Creek, not far from the church.

"I knew my husband all my life. We were both reared in the same neighborhood and went to school together. When we married, we didn't have a wedding—just came to Athens and got married at my cousin's house. Her husband was a preacher.

"My husband worked for the Athens Railway and Electric Company, now the Georgia Power Company. He started to work for them when he was fifteen years old and was still in their service at the time of his death eleven years ago. He started working for them as an errand boy until he learned what to do; then when the plant was built, they gave him a regular job making ninety dollars a month.

"When he was made plant manager he made $165 a month. My husband didn't go to war because he was operating the power plant. We had been married eleven years when he died. I have four children—two girls and two boys.

"The day he was killed at the plant at Tallassee [on the Oconee River] where we were transferred from Barnett Shoals in 1926, we had just returned from a two-weeks vacation. The children were cross and sleepy, so I told him I would give them a bath, put them to bed, and after I got the house in order I would go to the plant and stay with him, as I often did.

"He agreed to this, as the boss from Atlanta was coming the next day on an inspection trip, and my husband wanted everything shining for them, as that was the orders his boss here had given him. I had just gotten the children to bed and was tying the sheet of soiled clothes to be sent to the wash woman the next day when the telephone rang and a man at the plant told me to come down quick—my husband had been hurt.

"I ran all the way, and he died soon after I got there. His death was caused from a broken insulator. The shock probably wouldn't have killed him, but he had been watering the grass and his shoes and clothes were damp.

"After his death, the company paid me fifty dollars a month until the Workman's Compensation was paid, which was about $3,600. After that was paid, they gave me a job looking after the property at Tallassee until the new plant was built and they put men out there. Then I had to look out for myself.

"I got twenty-five dollars a month, a house to live in and lights and water furnished free. They let me live in that house now. That is the reason I don't move to town.

"The first year I took charge after my husband's death, and paddling my own canoe I made eighty-five dollars that year selling milk, butter, chickens and eggs. I was out of work from December, 1937, until March of 1938.

"Did I try everywhere to find work! I asked everyone I knew for a job. Many a day I have gone back home wondering where to try next. Finally one day I went to the Welfare Office, asked for work and they sent me to the sewing room.

"What a revelation that was to me. That was my first job on WPA, and if it wasn't for the government work, I don't know what people like us would do. In this day and time you can't get office work to do or even a job as saleslady. The people employing help want young attractive people with pep and energy.

"My work at the sewing room was very pleasant; however I didn't stay there very long before I was transferred to another project paying more. I was there from March until July. I was sent to the Housekeeping Aide Project as an aide, and in October of last year I was made supervisor of the project."

Tallassee Dam foundation structure. *Photo credit:* Historic American Engineering Record, Library of Congress, taken in 1984.

Someone knocked on the office door. Mrs. Harris answered it: "Good morning, what can I do for you this morning?"

"Good morning," said the visitor. "Carson is my name. I work over here at the University at the barn. I heard about your work and thought I would investigate about getting a nurse to wait on my wife and son. My wife has been sick since Christmas. Now my son has come down sick and I need some help.

"I went to the Welfare Office and they sent me to you," he explained.

"Where do you live?" asked Mrs. Harris.

"Over on Ag Hill."

"That is the address?" she asked.

"Tain't got none 'cept Ag Hill."

"Well, you take this blank to the Welfare Office and they will fill it out for you and you bring it back to me. Then I will see what I can do for you," Mrs. Harris said.

He left, but was back in a few minutes.

"Say, lady, I took this slip where you told me to. I didn't get to talk to the one you told me to. As a big head lady was coming out the office, she took the paper, read it and told me to give it back to you—they didn't have nothing to do with it."

"All right, just give it to me and I will look after it for you, as there was a misunderstanding on the part of the person with whom you talked."

He started to leave. With the door open and his hand on the door knob, he turned back and stuck his bald head through the open door.

"Look here, lady, if you want a recommendation, just call Sheriff Jackson. He will tell you all you want to know about me. I am a deputy sheriff of this county, I have a daughter working here in town. My son has been working for the city, and I have a daughter working in Atlanta.

"I have been working all my life and married when I was seventeen years old. This is the first time I have ever asked for help before. We need somebody right away. The bills have piled up on me so since Christmas. It has got me down, and I would appreciate anything you can do for me," he said.

"Now, you must remember, Mr. Carson—our aides are not nurses. They do practical nursing and look after the home while the mother or whoever is in charge of the home is not able to see after it."

"I understand, but I need somebody bad and would like to have them today," he said.

He left, and Mrs. Harris was silent a few moments. "Now, I don't see why they can't hire someone to do the work. However, when a case is reported, we have to investigate whether it's a worthy one or not.

"You know, this is one way I think the government is spending their money that really is worthwhile. Of course, all the projects are worthwhile, or they wouldn't have been created.

"But this one helps humanity in more ways than one. It gives us work, and in doing this it helps others who are not able to help themselves.

"We have eight workers most of the time. Seven of them are white and we have one Negro helper.

"This Negro is a practical nurse. She hadn't had a job in months when she was put on this project, and was only on the job a day-and-a-half when she got outside work to do, making fifteen dollars a week. She worked two weeks. When a person gets outside employment, which we are supposed to do, they are automatically dropped from the project.

"If by any reason they lose their job, then they are taken back again after the case is thoroughly investigated.

"As I have already stated, this project was created to help those who are not able to help themselves, and to make living conditions in the home worthwhile. You know yourself when you are in the dumps and everything goes wrong, all we need is a friendly pat on the back to help us along, and that is the objective of WPA.

"We train these women on the project to go into homes where the families are not able to hire help when they are sick, to have their work done. They do practically everything there is to be done, except the family washing and heavy scrub work. Of course, you know yourself if you had illness in your home and no one to help you, and there were several small children—you wouldn't have time for that sort of work.

"They clean house, cook, sew or mend, if it is necessary, care for the children as well as cooking the proper food for the family and patient, and they do wash the patients' clothes.

"In fact they do everything a nurse and housekeeper does, but giving medicine—that is not allowed.

"Then after the mother is well again—before the aide leaves— meals are planned by the aide, showing them how to cook to get the best food value.

"You know, some people cook their food all day—in that case the food isn't fit to eat. We also teach children as well as the grown-ups how to eat at the table, also how to set the table and serve a meal, as well as to keep a clean, neat house.

"We also encourage them to be clean with themselves; however, there are people who won't do any better, no matter how much you talk to them.

"After the aides leave a home, they drop in for a friendly chat, just to see how their plans are progressing. It is remarkable to find the improvement in some homes but very discouraging to go into the homes of those who don't have any pride whatsoever.

"We have a group meeting of the workers in my office once a week. We get an outsider to talk to us—sometimes it's the head of the Red Cross here in town. She tells us how to make bandages, make beds and care for the sick. We also have our Clarke County Home Demonstration Agent to give us a talk on how to prepare food for the sick, as well as for the children. They also discuss how to set the table and table manners. You would be surprised how little some people know about such things.

"I didn't know as much as I thought I did myself about lots of things I have learned since I came on this project.

"We had a group meeting one day, presided over by our Home

Demonstration Agent, talking about how to care for the home, food, setting the table and manners. One of the workers was so impressed she went home and began with the children and up to her mother—teaching them the nice ways of doing in the home.

"Now it's attractive as it can be, considering what she has to do with in her home. The other night I got so mad at my oldest son. He came rushing in without washing his face and hands. He went to the table, grabbed up his cup of coffee without sitting down to the table.

"I said, 'Son, why don't you sit down and eat like you ought to instead of gobbling your food up like a hog?' He said, 'Oh, Mama, I ain't got no time to fool with table manners—hang with it, I have got to go.' And off he went. Now you know that wan't the way for him to act.

"One way we made money for our project, as our sponsors did not supply any for it, is this: I made marmalade at night and the aides sold it after they got off from work. However, we didn't make a great deal, but it did give us a little to carry on in our project.

"This money was used to buy provisions for demonstrations we have once a week in teaching the aides how to prepare diets for sick people. Most of our food is furnished by the commodities.

"We have a loan closet. Most of the linen was donated by the aides. However, several organisations have given a few sheets, pillow cases and gowns. These things are loaned to the sick attended by our aides. When the patient is well again, these things are taken up, laundered and put back in the closet.

"You know, lots of people don't have what they need. and these things have to be provided for them.

"One day a case was reported, so I went to investigate it. I found a widow with two children. She and one of the children were sick in bed. There was no one to do anything for them, but a man she had hanging around. She called him her boy friend.

"We went in that home and took the woman and child in charge. We cleaned the house, washed their clothes and cooked their food.

"The man never left. We got tired of him staying there, doing nothing while we waited on him, too. The woman didn't realize he didn't care anything for her—only to eat up what she had, and a place to sleep.

"I put him to work cleaning the yard and burning trash. So the next day I made him scrub floors. Each day we gave him a different job. He soon got tired of working and left. Of course we had to get rid of him in a nice way, so she wouldn't get mad with us about it, and not let him know what we were up to.

"The aides wear white uniforms, and go quietly about their work in the home, just like any nurse would do. It is strictly against the rules to relate anything they see and hear, other than what they go to do.

"One of the most pitiful cases we have on record, is a blind woman who lives alone, and as far as we can learn, she has no relatives living in town or any other place.

"Her house was very good, but the interior was terrible to see. This case was reported to us, so one day one of the aides went to the house, and found the blind woman in bed, sick. She did not have any food in the house and hadn't had anything to eat in several days.

"The aide went in and did everything that was necessary. She has been on the case two weeks. Every day before she leaves, the aide brings in wood to make a fire, brings in coal and puts it in reach, so if the woman should have to get up in the night she won't hurt herself or take cold going out for it.

"The aide also places her food and water on a table by the bed.

The doctor told us this one case alone was worth all the money spent in the county from this project.

"There was an old woman who didn't have anyone but two boys to wait on her. They didn't even have a change of sheets, or the proper clothes. So we got clothing and food for them, as well as caring for her a long time.

"We went back to that home to see how they were getting on, and you wouldn't know it—there was such a change! At first the yard was littered with everything under the sun. When we went back, the yard and house was as neat and clean as could be.

"There was clean cover on the beds, a clean cloth on the eating table and a flower pot in the center of it. Things like that makes us know our work is worthwhile.

"Our work is very interesting, but since our project is not such an old one, I believe I have told you all of any importance. I have heard of people in other places having doors slammed in their face, water thrown on them, as well as being cursed out, but that has never happened to us.

"People we have dealt with are only too glad to have us go into their homes and help them," she said.

Her son came in: "Mama, we will have to get a new cross-member for that car."

"Well, I can't get it fixed today." his mother replied.

"Yes, you can, and I have to have a new wheel too. It shimmies so I can't hold it in the road," the son complained.

"Well, you ought not to have run it in the ditch and broke it." she said.

"You know I couldn't help it—the road was slick. The garage man said he will sell me a wheel cheap," he told his mother.

"I reckon he will, but I need to buy a pig to fatten so we will have some meat to eat next winter. Did you see any pigs this morning?"

"Naw, I didn't look for none."

"You had better go back to school," Mrs. Harris told him.

"I ain't going to no school today. I want the car fixed."

"Hush about that car—it will run a few days longer," she told him.

I asked him, "Where do you attend school?"

"At the University High," he answered.

Turning to her son, she said, "I want you to mail these letters."

"I ain't going to mail no letters, 'less you have the car fixed," he said.

"As soon as I can, I will," she said. "I need it now in my work. I have got to go 'way on the other side of town. Since it isn't raining, I will have to walk.

"Now, go on. I am busy and can't take up any more time today. I have other things to do."

The last thing her son said was: "Well, I am going, but ain't you going to have the car fixed today?"

A Day in a Store:
The Southern Department Store

Editor's Note: Writer Grace McCune did the interviews recounting a day at the Southern Department Store on Jan. 24, 1939. She interviewed Abe Link, the store manager; and clerks Mrs. Maude Elliott, Mrs. B. F. McEntire, and Mell McCurdy. The store was at 312 E. Broad St. in downtown Athens. The 1938 Athens City Directory showed Abraham Link living at 362 Cloverhurst Ave., and listed him as the department store manager. He was married to Mabel V. Link. The Link family was listed at the same address in the 1942 directory, but was not shown in later directories.

No information has come to light concerning Abe Link's subsequent residences or when he died.

Maude Elliott, called "Maud" in the Southern Department Store interviews, was listed as Mrs. Maude N. Elliott, living at 215 E. Dougherty, in the 1938 city directory. Mrs. B. F. McEntire was listed in the 1938 directory as Annie L. McEntire, widow of B. F. McEntire, and was living at 185 Baxter St. Mell "McCurrdy," as he was termed in the interview, was listed in the 1940 directory as Ernest M. McCurdy, a salesman at the department store, living in Comer, Georgia, in Madison County.

• • •

It was in a cold, drizzling rain that I made my visit to a very popular department store. It was such a disagreeable day that few people would get out unless it was necessary for work or business, and thinking this would be a good day to get a story, I went early.

As I opened the door, I was hailed by the store workers, wanting to know how I ever got out of a nice, warm office to come down there on such a day. I told them, the same thing that brought them out was the cause of my getting out, also. They were ordering Coca-Colas, and I was invited to join them.

As we were finishing our drinks, Mr. Link, the manager, came in and wanted to know why we picked such a cold day for cold drinks. The store is heated by a large circulating heater in the center of the first floor.

They were all around the heater waiting for the store to get warmer before they started their work of dusting counters and straightening stock. They were all talking about their different work. One clerk has the dry goods department, which is on the first floor; a man is the one that has charge of the shoes and men's clothing, which is also on the first floor; another clerk is saleslady in the ladies' ready-to-wear and millinery department. This is located in a balcony that covers half of the first floor.

As they went about their work, Mr. Link said, "You know that this building is one of the oldest brick buildings in Athens, and it was built when Broad Street was the main street in town. It is three stories: our department store has the first floor, the Joel Brothers, Jake, a lawyer, and Charles have their offices on the second floor.

"On the third floor is an overall and work-shirt plant. This plant was owned by the Joel brothers, but they have sold it to another company.

"It was in this building that Michael Brothers first started in business, and I think their home at that time was down on Oconee Street. Next, Louis Morris had a dry goods store here for some years, and then it was bought by old man Abe Joel. He is dead now, but the building is still owned by his sons.

"Joels were in business here for years, until the old man's health got bad and he sold out his store to my father-in-law. He has also passed away. The Joel boys then opened up the overall plant on the third floor, and ran it up until last year when they sold out to another company.

"We moved to Athens when I was about nine, and I have been here since that time. I went to school here, graduated from the University of Georgia. I worked for my daddy's store, here on Broad Street, also, while I was going to school. Those were great days—the boys don't hit it as hard now as we did then.

"I remember one night when the freshmen were having a banquet, the sophomores were trying to prevent the freshmen from attending. I was carried out below Princeton and tied out on the riverbank to a tree. They told me that they would come back for me after the banquet was over, but if I should by any means be able to get away from the tree, I would be allowed to attend without any more trouble from them, and they left me there.

"It was getting night, and I couldn't work those ropes loose. Finally I heard an old man over on the hill. He had been ploughing and was hollering at his mule, and that old 'gee-haw, whoa mule, gee-haw' sure sounded good to me.

"Thinking he would help me, I started yelling as loud as I could. He heard me and came to see what was the trouble. I begged him to untie me. He wanted to know what I would give him. I promised him a new pair of shoes if he would come to Dad's store the next day. He cut the rope and I lit out for home.

"Yes, I had to walk, but who minded that if we could out-do the sophomores. And I just knew I could get in now and they would not bother me any more that night. I went home, bathed and dressed in my tuxedo, even had the high silk top hat. I was feeling great, but it didn't last.

"I went strutting along, head high in the air. As I reached the old Imperial Hotel, where the banquet was being held, the sophomores were all lined up. As they saw me, they wanted to know how in the hell I got away. I pulled off the high top hat and made a most polite bow to them. But, oh, boy, I paid for that, despite that gentlemen's agreement that when a freshman managed to work out of any place they put him he was free to go where he wanted to.

"They threw rotten eggs all over my clothes and especially my nice high, top hat. I was ruined. They wouldn't let me inside with all those rotten eggs on me. I finally managed with the help of one of my friends to get out of my clothes, and he got up a couple of aprons and tied around me. That is how I attended the banquet, but at that some of them were worse off than I was."

At this time, an old Negro woman came in, wanting to see the manager. He asked her what he could for her.

She said, "Now just look right hyar at dis pair of shoes; dey done busted plum out, and I jist got 'em Saddy nite."

Looking over the pair of felt house slippers, he said, "Aunty, didn't you get them a little too small?"

The answer came right back, "I didn't git 'em a-tall—my gal done buyed 'em fer me."

Mr. Link laughed and told the shoe salesman to give her a new pair of house shoes. She thanked him and said, "I done tole 'em dat you would make 'em good."

Two Negro men came in wanting to see some overall jumpers. The clerk took them to the back of the store where the overalls were, and they first wanted to see some "dat had linin' in 'em."

But after they had looked at every one of them, they wanted to see "some of dem dat warn't lined a-tall."

They were shown these and told the prices of both. After examining both kinds for some time, they decided the sizes weren't right and they would look around somewhere else. As they departed, the clerk said, "That is what clerks go all through the day. Why sometimes I meet them at the door and ask if I can help them and they will walk all over the store and out again, without even answering me at all. Then sometimes they will walk around and then finally ask if we have a rest room.

"We have all kinds of experiences in our work, but we also have some very nice customers, and most of them are nice. And it is a pleasure to wait on them.

A woman came in looking for a hand bag to match a suit. The clerk helped make the selection, also showing gloves to match the bag. The customer thanked her, as she paid for them, saying, "You have been so nice to take up so much time with me."

After selling a man some children's socks, then selling a woman a child's sweater and cloth to another customer, she came back to answer the telephone. It was someone who wanted some of the clerks to go out on the street to see if they couldn't find a dray, and be sure and get one that had a good horse and wagon.

I asked if they had many calls like that, and she said, "Why all the time. When it is not bad weather, there are usually both drays and trucks around on Jackson Street, and some people think we have time to hunt up a dray anytime they want one."

A small, well-dressed man came into the store and asked for Mr. Link. The man introduced himself as Mr. Jacobson. He said he was from Florida and on his way to Hot Springs at his doctor's suggestion, and needed some help to get there.

Mr. Link asked him how long he had been sick. He said, "For sometime. I am not accustomed to asking for help, but I spent everything I had trying to get well. I have always donated highly to our society for the help of Jews, and it is embarrassing now to have to ask for help myself. But I just can't stay here in this weather, for it will put me right back in bed."

Mr. Link asked if he had been to the president of their [the Jewish] society in Athens. He said, "Yes," and that the president gave him a place to stay the night before, but that was all he could do for him. Mr. Jacobson then called the president of the Sisterhood. She refused to do anything at all for him.

He asked her if he should get sick here, who should he refer to—her or the Rabbi. He thanked her very politely, placed the telephone back on the desk and said, "I have never had anyone to talk to me that way before. Why, she said that if I should get sick to call on the city, that they were supposed to take care of folks like me. Well, when I had plenty of money I had plenty of friends."

Asking who the Rabbi was and where he lived, Mr. Jacobson went out. A salesman came in to see the manager, saying he had his new samples of ladies' underwear and a lovely line of ladies' blouses, both wash and silk, sport and for dress wear, in all the new shades that went with the new spring suits.

Mr. Link asked the clerks if there was anything in this line that they needed. But they said that they had already placed their orders. The salesman wanted to know why he was never able to land an order from them.

They said. "Well, you are always too late."

The salesman said business wasn't as good with him this trip, and that he didn't think anyone made any money last year, and were lucky to break even. Mr. Link told him that the fall of the year was when he did his best business, for his largest buyers were farmers, but that it was very disappointing last fall. The farmers had short crops, did not make anything, depended too much on their cotton and lost on that.

"And when the farmers fail, I lose also, as they do not have the money to spend," he said.

Two colored men came in and wanted to see some men's underwear. The clerk asked if they wanted the union suits. Hesitating, one of them said, "Yasser, dat's it."

They were shown a heavy weight suit, which was too heavy. The light weight was too light "fer wuk."

Nothing was just right, and they left to look around, saying, "If us don't find 'em, den us'll sho' be back."

A girl came in and asked to see an umbrella. Mr. Link waited on her, as the others were busy. She asked for an oil skin, but when he showed those, she wanted a cellophane one. After looking at these, and also the cloth ones, she finally decided on the oilskin.

Then she wanted to know if he had any rubber overshoes. He got out the old-time overshoes and she asked if she should try them on over her wet Oxfords, or if she would have to take her shoes off.

Mr. Link told her that he could not fit them on her feet, for then they wouldn't fit the shoes. After working to get them on over the wet shoes, she said she would take the umbrella and come back later for the overshoes, and be sure and put them aside for her. As she went out, he told the clerk that if she came back to give her the 8 1/2, for she would never get the size 8 on her feet.

She also wanted to know: if she just wore the overshoes without the shoes would they look any smaller?

Two Negro girls entered. They were met by the clerk, who asked if she could help them. They just walked by her, went up to the ready-to-wear department. The clerk up there met them at the top of the steps with the same polite offer to help them. They walked by her, looked at hats, pulled out dress racks, looked at them, then walked out of the store without speaking at all.

The clerk downstairs finished waiting on some more customers, and said it was time for her to go to lunch. As she started out the door, she was met by the husband of one of her old customers. His wife wanted some cloth matched and no one could do it but her, so she came back and waited on him and then she went on for lunch.

I went up to the ready-to-wear department. Two Negro women were looking at a child's wash dress. One said it would take one size, but the other insisted on a smaller size. Finally, arguing, they bought the dress, then wanted to see the hats. The clerk was very considerate and showed the new hats which had just come and explained the different styles and colors. One of them picked up a small roll brim hat and said, "ain't dis pretty? I sho' does lak it, and I sho' am coming back and git dis very hat."

The clerk asked if they wouldn't like to see some of the new spring dresses and especially the new suits. One of the women opened a box she had and showed a new suit that she had just bought for $6.95 and wanted to know if their suits were as nice as the one she had just bought.

Assuring the woman that she had suits just that nice, the other then said she was coming back to the Southern Department Store for her suit. As they went out, the clerk said, "It is all in a day's work.

"My motto is to do unto others as I would like to have them do for me, and I don't try to sell anyone else something that I would not want myself. I try to treat everyone fair in every way, and I do appreciate my customers. I have built up a good business with them. Most of them are nice and considerate; of course we have some that are trying. But I can wait on them for hours and know that they are not going to buy.

"Only the other day, I sold a woman a coat. It was a hard sale, as she did not know just what she wanted, but after I had put it in the box and handed it to her, she said, 'I just reckon as how I won't take it.' It took another good hour to sell her the coat all over again.

"And then I had another customer that I showed everything in this department, and everything I showed her, she said, 'Ma has got one just like it.'

"Very often these young flappers come in and try on dresses and hats just to have a place to smoke and rest, but they are usually very nice.

"One day a lady came and wanted to see my very latest dresses. After trying them all on and examining them to see how they were made, she said, 'I thank you very much. I am a dressmaker and I just wanted to see how the new styles looked. It will give me new ideas in my work.'

"Some people think that clerks have an easy job, but they don't realize that we have to keep this stock in place and that it has to be brushed and dusted every day, and it takes hours to get it fixed back after a busy day.

"Then every season things have to be packed away to make room for the new things and I wonder every year as I pack and put away things if I will be here next year to unpack them.

"I have worked on this same block for twenty-seven years," she said.

I asked her to tell me about it. She laughed and said, "Well, I will tell you what I can. I was young when I went to work right in this same store for Mr. Abe Joel.

"I had never worked before, and I was started in at five dollars a week, but that was big money to me. I worked two weeks; then I was called to the office. I just knew I had done something wrong and my knees were shaking so I could hardly walk. But when I got there, they told me that I had tried hard to learn, and they were satisfied with my work, and they were raising my salary to ten dollars a week.

"We worked hard, but business was good then and didn't have so much competition. Farmers would come in to buy, and they bought for the whole family and the bills amounted to something.

"We always got a bonus check at Christmas, for Mr. Joel and the boys gave us a piece of gold money."

She had to stop and wait on some customers and I looked around her department. One side was filled with dress racks full of dresses, and in the center of the balcony were several large round dress racks, one of house dresses at 98 cents, one rack at $1.98, one at $3.95. All dresses run from 98 cents to $7.95.

Suits were at different prices—popular prices in tailored suits were $9.90. Coats light and heavy weight at different prices, rain coats, $1.98 to $2.98. Children's dresses from 49 cents up. The other side was hats, all sizes, colors and shapes. On a table in the center floor was displayed a nice line of hats that were priced at 98 cents.

The better hats were in showcases and in the hat shelves. A large glass case also held blouses, gloves, and handbags, sport shirts and uniforms. These were all priced from 98 cents to $1.98, and some a little higher.

The sewing room and fitting room were in the rear, and in the fitting room was a table, chair and a long mirror. The sewing room had a long sewing table with an electric machine, an ironing board and electric iron, a long table with a mirror over it, and the room was heated by a small heater.

There was also a large full-length mirror in the main part of the balcony for trying hats and dresses.

At one side was the cashier's stand, where the baskets came from all parts of the store, as the cashier also wrapped the packages. This cashier stand is used only in the busy season, as they had a register and wrapping counter on the first floor.

As the clerk finished with her customers, she came back to me, and said, "Did you know that I have had two weddings right here on my balcony? But that was when I was working for Mr. Joel. I dressed both the brides.

"The first couple was from the country, and the bride came in and bought her outfit, from underwear to shoes and hat. We dressed her in the fitting room, and they called a Justice of the Peace to marry them. I never laughed so much in my life, for he asked the groom if he would take the bride and feed her on cornbread and collards. Of course, all the clerks as well as our other customers were watching and listening. And I thought they would laugh themselves to death when the Justice of the Peace asked that question.

"The next wedding we had was really a nice wedding. It was a couple from Madison County. We dressed that bride, also. They had some of their friends with them and we called Preacher Elliott to marry them, and it was quite different from the first one.

"Mr. Joel could just think of everything and did things so different from anyone else. One year, business was bad. Farmers had a bad year and couldn't get anything for their cotton and couldn't pay their bills. Mr. Joel bought a bale of cotton and put it out in front with a big sign on it saying, 'We will buy your cotton at ten cents a pound.'

"He would buy the farmers' cotton, and we sure did do business that fall, for they all traded with him, and paid their bills with the cotton they couldn't sell. In this way we did a good business, kept our old customers, and made many new ones.

"When the war came, his two oldest sons were just the age to go. They volunteered. We all hated to see them go, and we knew just how it hurt Mr. Joel, but he did not want his boys to be slackers. We just tried that year to see how hard we could work.

"Business was good everywhere then and we sure got our part. At Christmas I received a bonus check for $300, with 'Merry Christmas' on it. He was a good man to work for, and he appreciated what his clerks did for him. I never had any trouble with him but one time. I came in one morning a few minutes late, and several customers were waiting for me. The boss gave me a dirty look and also a raking over before my customers.

"That made me mad. I went ahead with my customers and, after they were gone, I went back to our dressing room, got my coat and hat, went by the office and told them that I was quitting, as I didn't intend to be treated any such a way before my customers—and I walked out.

"Mr. Joel called me, but I didn't stop. I had just reached my home when two of the boys got there. They talked to me and begged me to come back. They told me what was wrong with their dad. One of the banks had closed that morning—he had several thousand dollars in the bank. He was worried and didn't realize that he was so cross. I stayed at home a week and went back and I never had any more trouble with him. I worked for him as long as he was in business. In fact, I worked for them fourteen years and ten months.

"After he went out of business, I worked for another store in this same block until 1932, and then I came back here to work for Mr. Link.

"But it is time for my lunch hour now—will you have lunch with me?"

I thanked her and told her I would get a sandwich later, as I wanted to talk to the other clerks while they were not busy.

As I went back to the first floor, two ladies came in the front door. The clerk met them, but they had just come in to warm and rest a while. She invited them back to the fire, and placing chairs for them, went to wait on another customer.

I listened to them talk while they rested. One said she "just had to come to town, and see 'bout gettin' something to fix" for her children's school lunch.

"You know I has three in school, and they has got to the place where they think they is too good to take jelly and butter and bread, or for that matter, they didn't want eggs, no preserves, neither.

"Just thinks they has to have fruits, sich as apples, oranges, and bananas, and why, if I didn't just set my foot down, they wouldn't take a thing 'cept candy.

"My children can eat really more than most grown folks, 'cause they ain't finicky 'bout what they eat at home. It is just what they takes for lunch."

The other lady said she had come "plum to town" to get her radio fixed.

"When they told me that it would take all of two hours' work to get it fixed, I decided to come down here to wait," she said. "I knowed they wouldn't mind—they all'ers have such good fires and are so nice to us when we wants to warm and rest.

"Why, sometimes folks eats dinner right here, when they has to be in town all day. 'Tain't no wonder that folks likes to trade here, and I try to do all my trading here. They are always nice.

"I bring them eggs 'most every time I come, and they always buy them and garden stuff, too, but I didn't have any today. My children all like eggs and they come in handy in fixing up their lunches.

"But they told me to be sure and bring back the radio. We all likes to listen to it at night when we are through work, but I'm glad they likes it for it keep them from gallivanting 'round so much at night."

The women then got to discussing the Bible and said folks didn't read it right and anyway no one understood it. After arguing this way and that way, they started out—one to see if by any chance her radio was fixed sooner than they said—and the other one to see if the boys 'warn't ready to go home,' and she still had to hunt for something else to help in lunches and she just had to be home by night.

The clerk came back to the fire then, and said, "It has been a good day for sweaters, for it is really cold outside. But I will tell you a joke on the boss."

Mr. Link had just come in and he said, "Now look here, if these folks are going to talk about the boss, just let me talk first, and tell you that my clerks are all so much older than I am that they have no respect for me and just talk to me any old way."

This brought a protest as well as a laugh and very friendly argument between the boss and clerks.

One of them said, "Just write that our boss was one of the best pitchers in soft baseball here for years, until Father Time stopped him, and now he plays golf."

Mr. Link laughed and said, "They will ruin me yet. Better let her tell her joke; for I know I will have to pay for it."

The clerk said, "Well, last week a lady came in to buy a sweater for another woman and said she wanted a 38, as the woman she was buying for was larger than she was.

"She didn't want anything except a dark blue. I know my stock pretty well and I knew that sweaters run small to the size. The lady that was buying couldn't have worn less than a 42. I gave her a 46 and told her that if it didn't fit I would exchange it or give her the money back.

"After she had gone, Mr. Link bet two Coca-Colas to one that she would bring it back, for it would be too large. And yesterday the lady came back. Mr. Link asked her how the sweater was, and she said it was just a perfect fit and the lady was well pleased."

I asked if the boss paid off. He answered before she could, said, "No," but he was going to, for if they ever got anything on him, he never heard the last of it. He said, however: "After all, they are pretty good sports and we have worked together so long that we don't mind each other.

"We have extra help on Saturdays, and in the fall we have several extra ones on the force. These long dull days just whips us all down. They are worse than being busy. We have a good trade among the farmers, but last fall was disappointing," he said.

"Farmers made short crops, depended on their cotton too much and the boll weevil ruined most all of that, and when the farmers fail then we all lose, too.

"Business was not so good last year, but we are expecting and looking forward to a better business this year, and I hope we will not be disappointed. We open at eight in the morning and close at six. Except on Saturday nights, when we stay open late for the benefit of our customers that have to work, also.

"Of course we come in contact with all classes and kinds of people. Most of them are nice, but we do run across many amusing things in our work. In the fall rush we have a young boy from the university to work with us. He is a fine boy and well liked by all in the store, but we get a good many laughs on him.

"Especially one time last fall. A lady from the country came in to get a pair of shoes. This boy was waiting on her, and he is very nice to his customers. He had tried on several pair, when all at once she wanted to know if he was a married man. He hardly knew how to answer, but told her that he was not married.

"She refused to let him finish waiting on her, said she was a married woman herself and she didn't want 'no young upstart fitting shoes on her feet.'

"She said if there weren't no married men that could try on her shoes, she would go 'sommers else.' An older clerk was called and after assuring her that he was married and had a large family, she let him fit her shoes and bought them," Mr. Link said.

Reminiscence
by Mrs. Leola T. Bradley

ও৩৺৶৩৶

Editor's Note: Mrs. Leola T. Bradley was born in Dublin, Laurens County, Georgia. She was a research field worker for the Georgia Writers' Project and in the 1938 Athens City Directory was shown living at 347 Hill St. The directory also lists her as the widow of L. D. Bradley, who is further identified in her manuscript as Louie D. Bradley.

She wrote about herself for the Life Histories, indicating she lived at 424 S. Lumpkin St. on Sept. 27, 1939, at the time she wrote the article. She was identified in the manuscript edited by Mrs. Maggie B. Freeman as being an ex-teacher and a WPA worker. Mrs. Bradley died at the age of seventy-seven on July 2, 1967, in Fulton County, Georgia.

Although not strictly an oral Life History, the self-interview is included for the information given about WPA activities and the background of one of the WPA workers in Athens.

• • •

My childhood was not very different from that of the average child. I was born down in Dublin, Laurens County, Georgia. My father was a pharmacist there for forty-five years. I was one of seven children—four brothers and two sisters.

My mother was one of the most devout Christians I have ever known. Father was a fine man, too, but somehow children, as a rule look more to the mother for spiritual guidance. There has never been a happier home than ours was. Large families are happier than small ones, I think.

We had our squabbles as most children do. Sometimes we were sad, then again we were glad. We loved a lot and fussed a lot. We lived comfortably but not luxuriously. Father did not believe in indulging children too much.

My father and mother were both musical, and with only one exception all of the children inherited that talent. When we were old enough to take music lessons, a piano was bought. Most of us had good voices, and we played not only the piano but also other instruments. We had an old organ that had been handed down to my father from generations back. We would gather around at night and sing to Mother's accompaniment.

I was the youngest girl, so my brothers and sisters thought I was the favorite, but I really don't think there was any preference shown.

Father, in those days did not believe in public schools, so along with three or four other families, we went to a private school.

Since I went to this private school, I did not have to wait until the required age to enter, so I began very early. After several years, we entered the public school, and as I was well advanced, I graduated very young.

I displayed a decided talent for music—at any rate every one thought so—and I was given every advantage both in piano and voice. I was too young, my parents thought, to go away to college so they decided to keep me at home a year.

Funny how little things can turn your whole life. One night I was in bed just recuperating from a cold, and the telephone rang. It was the school superintendent under whom I had graduated. He had been called over long distance by a superintendent of a school in a neighboring town, asking him to recommend a music teacher.

Their teacher had run away and married. Well, to make a long story short, I went down there to finish out the term. Never did any one feel so little and helpless as I did when I started out on my first job.

I never will forget my trip down to that place. I went on the train and though it was only a short distance, I had to change trains at a little junction. Well, much to my dismay when I reached this junction, my train had left me. There was nothing to do but spend the night. I knew the depot agent's wife, so he took me to his home for the night.

To go back a little, I tried to dress myself up to look the part of a dignified teacher. I had a hat with a feather on it, of which I was very proud. That night we went up the street to visit some friends. When we returned, there were feathers—feathers all over my room.

The cat had gotten hold of my cherished hat and torn the feathers completely up.

The next morning, we got up, found some ribbon and fixed my hat, and I went on my way, reaching my destination around eleven o'clock.

In a small town everyone was curious to know how the new music teacher was going to look. I learned this later.

As no one met me at the train, I walked up the street to the little hotel, which was only a short distance. On my way I passed two men who scrutinized me rather closely—not rudely, but in an interested sort of a way. They were not old as we term age today but were considerably older than I—nice looking, well dressed. I hurried by, but unfortunately I dropped my bag. As I paused to pick it up, I heard this remark.

"You can have her, Drew. I'm not running a kindergarten."

I did not dare look back to see which one made this remark, but it wasn't long before I found out. Well, anyway, he changed his mind before the year was out. Five years later we were married.

I did not accept a teacher's place the following term, for I wanted to go to college. In September, I went away to a college and conservatory of music in Mississippi. People wondered why I didn't go to one of our fine Georgia Schools, but there were several reasons. One was, I was given a scholarship. Then, too, after the first year I was given a tutor's place in the Conservatory and helped pay my own way through school. I went there four years, and the last term I was a full-fledged teacher. I was young to be on the faculty, but I have always been a hard worker and conscientious, so I think I made good.

During that time I was also studying. The third year I was there I took my A.B. degree and my B.M. degree, majoring in voice. The fourth year I took a B.M. degree, majoring in piano.

I had promised Mr. Bradley I would marry him as soon as I finished college, but when I came home that summer, my mother begged me so hard to stay at home with her a year, I did. I felt that I was due her that much.

Mr. Bradley didn't like it much, but he couldn't do anything about it, so he waited.

I was elected to teach piano and voice in my home town school, so in that way, I could work and still be with my mother. My fiancé was not very far away, in the little town where I had done my first teaching, so I got to see him several times a week.

I've never regretted staying with my parents that year. I was really too young to marry anyway.

The following June I was married. I won't say that my married life began with the very brightest outlook—that is too broad a statement, but I do know it seemed to me I was the happiest creature on earth. I just wondered if it would last.

Well, in one respect it did. It was not unmixed with clouds, adversities and disappointments. We all have those if we live long enough. Our love was the one bright star that was never dimmed. But there, I'm getting ahead of my story.

Mr. Bradley was a big merchant in a small town. He had only

a high school education, but his many years of experience had taught him more, perhaps, than he ever would have learned in books. He was a number of years older than I. He loved home, and at mealtime and at night he loved to be there.

People thought we would not be congenial, for while I loved my home, I was not quite so settled in my ways. Those things adjusted themselves.

He did not know one note from the other, nor could he carry a tune, but he learned to love opera and other cultural things as well as I did. In other words, the longer we lived together, the more congenial we became.

Our first baby, a girl, was born when we had been married about two-and-a-half years. That same fall we made enough to finish paying for our business. He did not have it entirely paid for when we married.

Our next goal was a home of our own. We were paying rent then. I was a little inclined to want a car first. Numbers of my young friends had them; but my husband insisted that a home was more important right then. In January, just as the World War broke out, we built our home. I see now, it was a mistake to have built the kind of home we did, in such a small place. I could not see what the future held for us. It never occurred to me, but that we would both always be there, and times would be just as prosperous as then.

Like most merchants, Mr. Bradley prospered during the war. Afterwards, though, there was a terrible slump in merchandising, and our business suffered a terrible blow.

We took it with a smile—we just cut down our mode of living, but were just as happy.

My husband was old-fashioned in his ideas of what women should and should not do. One night he came home from work with a part-cross and part-hurt expression on his face. I was worried, for he was usually in a good humor.

I didn't say anything—just waited for him to speak.

"Well." he said, "I was certainly hurt and surprised at something I heard this afternoon."

"Why, what have I done?" I said.

"I never thought the time would come when my wife would take part in politics."

Well, I didn't vote that year. After that, his views began to change, and soon he was taking me to the polls every election day. I don't take any active part in politics, but I vote my convictions. I think every woman should do that. I am interested in public affairs, but I don't go wild over elections like some people. Of course, I think we all get a 'kick' over seeing our man go in.

I didn't do any work outside of my home the first years of our married life. It wasn't necessary from a financial standpoint. My husband thought I had plenty to do, to look after our home and little girl. I took an active part in church affairs.

I am naturally religiously inclined and was reared in that kind of atmosphere. I kept up my music, especially voice. I did lots of club work, too. At one time I was first District Director in the Georgia Federation of Music Clubs. So, even though I lived in a very small country town, my activities were not confined to my environment.

My husband was unusual in this respect—he was very ambitious about my voice. Not many men would consent for their wives to leave them and go away for three months at a time to study. Well, he did, and not only that, he gave me the money.

He knew that I had been accustomed to a larger town and felt that I needed a change. So instead of taking just pleasure trips each summer, I would go away to study. One summer I spent in Atlanta. I had only one child then, so I took a little apartment and kept house for three months.

Mr. Bradley spent his vacation with us and also came up for weekends. I look back on that as being one of the happiest summers of my whole married life. I studied under Miss Lull Clark King. She is still teaching in Atlanta. She helped me lots.

The next summer I went to the American Conservatory of Music in Chicago. I continued my voice lessons and also studied Public School Music. The following summer I completed that course. I don't consider any musical education complete now without Public School Music—in fact, even school teachers now have to know how to teach it.

After I completed this course in Chicago, I began going to the University of Georgia summer school. That was during the time when the university had such a fine school of music. They had one whole week during each summer devoted to grand opera, concerts, etc.

The best of talent was assembled here for that week. It was truly a gala occasion. Mr. George Fulsome Granary of New York was director of the School of Music, and also directed Opera. He was nice to me. and I feel that I owe more to him than any musician I have ever contacted. He gave me outstanding parts in Opera. That helped to broaden my musical career more than all the study I had received.

I kept that up for seven consecutive summers. Sometimes, I would feel badly over spending so much money on myself, but the time came later in life when I was truly glad that I had not spent my time in idle pleasure.

We were a little disappointed that our family was so small, for we still had one child. I like large families when you can give them what they need to become good citizens. Just as we had resigned ourselves to just one child, along came a little boy. No need to tell you we were happy, we were just thrilled to death. We named him Louie for his father.

About that time I began to realize that finances were getting bad. Mr. Bradley said little about it, but I knew he was worried, although he tried to hide it. Our business had never quite recovered from the depression following the war.

I had had several opportunities to help out the family budget by teaching, but my husband would not consent on account of the children.

I was soon to find out that life was not always to be as carefree as it had been so far. When our boy was one year old, he was stricken with colitis in its worst form. I nursed him, with the help of friends, for four weeks.

He began to get better, but was in a terribly weakened condition. Then he developed double pneumonia. I felt that we could never pull him through that, but we did.

The Lord certainly must have spared him for some good purpose. I don't know yet, for in some respects, he has had one of the saddest lives of any child I've ever known.

Well, troubles never come singly. Since then my life has been full of adversities. Before Louie had regained his strength, our little girl, Mary, was rushed to a neighboring town for an emergency appendix operation. All this sickness was a terrible strain on us, mentally, physically and financially.

When Mary was able to return home from the hospital. Little Louie was on the road to recovery. We thought surely our troubles were over for a while.

One afternoon a short time later, I was on the porch with the baby, when two ladies drove up to the house. They introduced themselves, told me they were looking for a voice teacher, and asked if I would consider taking them.

"Well," I said, "I have taught a good bit in my life, but not lately."

I then told of all the sickness I had had, and what a care my children were. They insisted, so I finally told them I would teach them.

They lived twenty miles away and were to drive over twice a week for their lessons. That was the beginning of my returning to my profession. Soon other pupils began coming, and in a short while I had all the pupils I could teach, right in my own home.

It was the wisest decision I ever made. too, for in November we lost our business. Mr. Bradley did a big credit business. That, along with the Depression, just ruined his. That left us about where we first started out. We had our home, though, and I was teaching, so we still felt that we had much to be thankful for.

Mr. Bradley soon got a job travelling, selling flour and food-stuffs. He didn't make anything like the money we had been ac-customed to having, but with my help we managed. Once more we thought our difficulties were over, for a while at least.

One night we were sitting at the supper table and all at once he began gasping for breath. His face was ashy-white. I ran to the phone, and soon the doctor was there.

I have never seen such suffering as my husband endured. The doctor sat by him all night, and just before dawn, he seemed to rest a little. He had angina pectoris and in the worst form. I be-gan to realize then what was before me—two children and a hus-band who could likely be taken from us at any time.

I was elected to teach piano-voice and public school music, in a school sixteen miles away. I knew it meant leaving my home and children a good part of the time, but I accepted the place. It seemed that some kind providence was coming to our rescue in every emergency. I taught there in the same school for seven years, commuting in my car.

Most of that time Mr. Bradley was not able to work and I was the only support. He helped me lots with the children. Mary, of course, was in school, but little Louie was not old enough, so he was his daddy's constant companion.

After about six months, my husband was able to go to work again. He bought out a small grocery store and things began to look brighter for us. Mary graduated from high school, and then there came the question of sending her to college. With the help of my husband's sister, we entered her at the University of Georgia. I brought her to Athens on Monday, September 25th.

The following Wednesday night she was called back. The death angel visited our home, taking the beloved husband and father. Even though I knew for several years he would probably go suddenly and at any time, I was not prepared for it. He dropped dead on his way home from work; little Louie and his dog were the only ones with him at the time.

Those were truly dark days for us, and for a while it seemed that I just could not take up life again. But I did, for I had my two children to live for and who had to depend on me for everything.

Mary returned to the university after a week, and I resumed my teaching. Louie had just entered school. That fall was the loneliest I ever spent, but we made the best of it. I took a couple in to board with us and that helped lots.

Mr. Bradley did not leave us a great deal. He had borrowed on his insurance, always hoping he would get in physical condition to take out more. But he never did. We owned our house, though, and had a few thousand in cash. I was not afraid of the future, for I felt capable of earning a living for my children.

Money takes wings, though, when sickness comes. When Mr. Bradley had been dead only three months, Louie was taken desperately ill—"pneumonia"—the doctor said. After a few days we noticed a slight swelling in his hip and he began complaining of pain. As soon as we could we got him to a hospital for an X-ray. Osteomylitis was the diagnosis, bone infection.

For six months it was a battle between life and death. Then, too, I was faced with the possibility of his being a cripple even if his life was spared.

Doctors, hospital, nurses, and operations played havoc with my little bank account, for I gave him the best attention I knew how. The strain was beginning to wear me out both physically and financially. I was trying to teach all day and stay with him at the hospital at night. I saw he was getting no better at that place, so with the help of friends, I got him to the Scottish Rite hospital at Decatur.

That was the saving of him. He was there for two years. They let me bring him home for Christmas, but I carried him right back. That is truly a wonderful place. It's true he was left a cripple, but had it not been for the Scottish Rite he would not be here now. He is still under their care. I have to carry him back at intervals for examinations. In another year he is scheduled for another operation on his hip. That is to try to lengthen his limb and correct his limping.

When he was dismissed from there, it seemed that there was nothing for me to do but give up my teaching and stay home with him. He was on crutches and had to have lots of special care. So I resigned my job. That's how it happens that I am not teaching today, I guess. You know when you once get out of your profession, it's hard to get back—especially at my age. There are so many teachers without jobs.

After Mary finished her second year at the University of Georgia, I decided to give her a secretarial course. I took her to Washington, D.C., and entered her at Strayers School. She lived with my brother. She was very lucky, for through influence of some political friends there, she got a job in three months' time.

It was only a short time, though, before she fell in love, almost at first sight, and married. That was a blow to me at first, but on second thought I was really happy over it. Then when I met her husband, I was even happier.

Yes, she married a fine man and into a fine family. Her husband's father is American Consul General in Leipzig, Germany. I feel so sorry for him now during this European crisis.

They have not been able to hear from his parents since early in August. That is off my subject, though.

Finances were getting so bad with me that on the advice of friends, I moved to Athens, Georgia. My idea was to open a boarding house. I thought I could do that and be at home with my crippled child, too.

Well, that's the last thing I should have done. I know how to keep a nice house and set a nice table, but I knew absolutely nothing about the financial side of it. I opened up a lovely place on Prince Avenue, and right there is where I lost the last of my little savings. The sad part is I even sold my little house in South Georgia and invested it. That, too, was gone.

Then I began losing my nerve and my health. My boy had several severe attacks of illness and that took more money. I saw there was no more boarding house for me, so I stored what I had in the way of furniture, sold part of it, and began looking for work.

As a last resort, I went down to the Welfare Office and was certified for WPA work. My sister-in-law took my boy for me and found a little boarding school and put him there until I could get work. He has to have good care.

My first WPA assignment came right out of a clear sky. I had given up hopes. Imagine my chagrin when I opened my slip and read "Library Project—book repairer, twenty-five cents per hour." Of all things in the world I had never done, mending a book was the most unthought of. I soon learned it to be very fascinating work. Just to make an old book to look like new was really worthwhile.

Anyway, I was learning something I never expected to know. It was hard work and not much pay, either, but it was honest. That project closed in two months.

From September 10th to January 3rd of this year, I was without work. I can hardly tell you how I managed. My boy did not suffer, though, for he was still in this little school. By the way, it is a Catholic School and they certainly do take good care of him. He learns rapidly down there.

You see, two years of his school life was spent in the hospital so he is behind in his studies.

The WPA is a wonderful plan, I think, to give employment to people who really need it. The greatest trouble with me is that it has not been continuous work. I get so behind with finances between jobs. Then, too, while no one expects a big salary on WPA, I would like to make enough to give my boy the necessities of life. His shoes alone cost me twenty dollars per pair, besides the fare to Atlanta to get them fitted.

My next WPA job began January 3rd of this year. It lasted six months, and the pay was better than on the first one. I liked that fine. I was a field worker on the Real Property Survey. We made two surveys of Athens.

At first I felt funny going into all kinds of places and contacting all sorts of people, but I got over that. I have to meet people, so on the job I certainly had a good opportunity and made a lot of friends. I was not accustomed to walking, either, but I learned to do that, too.

Since working on that survey I feel that I know every nook and corner of Athens.

That job closed and I was wondering what I would do next. It seemed for six weeks that I wouldn't do anything. Again unexpectedly came another slip assigning me to what was then called the Federal Writers' Project. Since then it has been changed to Georgia Writers' Project.

I like it very much, especially the interviews and the research work. As for my writing—well I'm trying, but I'm afraid those people in Atlanta think I'm hopeless.

I think President Roosevelt is a wonderful man in many, many respects—especially his conceiving the idea of helping the unemployed. I appreciate the work, but of course I prefer private employment, and I am striving for it all the time.

There are other WPA jobs I might be better suited for. Music is my profession and of course I prefer something that I can do well. In other cities, I understand, there are projects for musicians. Athens does not have one, however.

My mode of living, of course, is not what it once was, but my ideals are just as high. Money does not mean everything, and even doing without luxuries does not kill. I attend church regularly, and when Louie is at home, he goes with me.

We are both members of the First Methodist Church and I sing in the choir there. I can't take any part in social functions any more nor in club work. I don't have the time or money, but those are not essentials anyway. My one ambition now is to see my boy grow into manhood, with just as high aspirations as his parents had.

George Shaw Crane

Editor's Note: George Shaw Crane, born in Clarke County, was a promi-nent Athens resident whose grandfather, Ross Crane, constructed early buildings on the University of Georgia campus. The Ross Crane house is a fine ante-bellum house which still exists as a fraternity house at Pulaski and Washington Streets.

George Shaw Crane was an outstanding football player for the Univer-sity of Georgia, lettering in 1893. He married Hallie Watkins in 1898. After her death, he married Mamie Davis in 1919. They lived for many years at 897 Prince Ave. after another home on Prince Avenue burned.

He died Oct. 22, 1962, in Athens at the age of eighty-seven, and his obituary called him one of Athens' best known and most highly-respected citizens.

Mrs. Sadie B. Hornsby interviewed the Cranes in sessions on Jan. 23, Jan. 26, and Feb. 1, 1939. Editing her interviews were Mrs. Sarah B. Hall of the Athens office and John N. Booth, area supervisor of the Federal Writers Project, in Augusta, Georgia.

• • •

"George Shaw Crane" was the name on the card above the electric button by the front door, and my ring was promptly answered by Mrs. Crane. She is a prim little woman, and on this occasion her neat, silk frock was protected by a print smock.

"Do come in, my dear," she said, with an inviting smile. My hostess left me in the living room, while she went to let her husband know that I was there. Glancing about me, I saw beautiful old furniture, some of which I later learned has been handed down from one generation to another in the Crane family for more then a hundred years.

A rare and lovely old, blue-glass carafe sat on the floor under a mahogany drop-leaf table that has been in this family since 1800. A mortar and pestle, given by Dr. Crawford W. Long, discoverer of anesthesia by ether, to a member of the Crane family, was placed on an interesting old bookcase.

Mr. Crane came in with his wife and invited me into the dining room.

"It's warmer in here," he explained, as we approached a glowing Franklin heater. When I explained that I had come to hear him tell his experiences in the renting business, he laughed heartily. "Why don't you ask Miss Mamie?"

"She could give you a much better story than I can, with all her experiences as a nurse before we married, and then, too, she knows as much about my renting business as I do—if not more. She's had many and varied experiences since she's been helping me keep our property rented."

"Oh, George!" she began, "You know how busy I am today. You just go ahead and talk. I'll be glad to help in any way I can, though. Just call me and I'll be right in."

"You'll find that dining table a good place to write on," said Mr. Crane, and as I opened my notebook, he continued the conversation.

"That table is what I would call a real antique. My grandfather Crane purchased it in 1800, and it has been in our family ever since. I myself, have eaten off of it sixty years. It's solid mahogany, and we have never had to have a thing done to it. Its construction is remarkable; there's not a nail in it.

"An expert spent four hours looking it over with a flashlight, and he declared that it wasn't made in America. He should know about good furniture, for he was apprenticed as a small boy to a manufacturer of fine furniture, and at the time he was in our home he was in his seventieth year.

"Practically all of his life has been spent in the furniture business. Another man offered me a complete dining room suite, the best obtainable, for this one table. Of course I refused the offer. That was in the days when all of us had plenty of money. I doubt if the man who made that offer could pay cash for a loaf of bread now."

Taking an odd-looking pistol from the mantel, Mr. Crane inquired, "Would you like to know the history of this?"

My knowledge of firearms is limited to almost nothing, and seeing the quizzical look with which I regarded the weapon, he answered the question that I had not voiced.

"Sure, it's a real pistol. Take it in your hands and see for yourself."

I begged him to tell me the story of the pistol. "Well," he said, "This was one of a pair of duelling pistols that my father used to keep in a handsome Morocco case in his desk. After our home burned in 1885, we found this one in the back yard, but we never did know what became of the other pistol and the case.

"These were the pistols used in the duel between Aaron Burr and Alexander A. Hamilton, and the one you see here now was the one fired by Burr to inflict the mortal wound. I suppose you remember reading that Hamilton died as the result of that duel. The pistols belonged to Hamilton, and were exactly alike, only the lost pistol was for a right-handed man. Aaron Burr was left-handed. If you held this one in your right hand, the hammer would obstruct your sight and endanger your marksmanship. But you can hold it in the left hand and sight from the small piece of steel on the right side of the barrel."

I had never known before that there was a time when a pair of pistols, like a pair of shoes, were made in "rights" and "lefts."

The University of Georgia 1893 football team. George Shaw Crane
lettered on the team and is first on the left, 2nd row.
Photo credit: Sports Communications, University of Georgia

"This pistol is of finest steel, and look at that handle! It's mahogany, I'm sure. Now, look closely and read the name of the
manufacturer, 'U. W. RICHARDS.' You remember, no doubt, that
Hamilton was an Englishman. How my father came into possession of them, I don't know."

Mr. Crane's ancestors have been connected with the develop-
ment of Athens from its pioneer days. His paternal grandfather
was the architect who designed some of the oldest of the many
notable buildings here, and his maternal grandfather was equally
distinguished.

Mr. Crane is rather stout, has black hair, and he seems to favor
a black broadcloth suit, black felt hat, black shoes, white socks,
white shirt and black tie to any other type of attire.

George Shaw Crane and Mamie Crane, with his first grand child.
Photo taken in 1954. *Photo credit:* Mrs. Francis Epps Crane Brame.

George Shaw Crane celebrates his
87th birthday in Athens.
Photo credit: Mrs. Frances Epps
Crane Brame

"Talking of buildings," said Mr. Crane, "I was born in New College on the Franklin campus of the University. Grandfather was one of the builders of New College, and 30 years after it was completed, while the University was closed because of the war, he and his family lived there. My mother was visiting them there when I was born.

"There were six of us boys, and we always realized what we missed not having a sister. We boys were into everything. In my young days all the houses were enclosed with picket fences, and we had our gateposts named 'twelve' and 'one.' When we had been out at night, next morning at the breakfast table our parents would ask us: 'What time did you boys come in last night?' 'Between twelve and one,' we always answered.

"We lived on this same street, down there in front of the church. The street was not laid out straight at that time like it is now. It was a part of the old stage route from Athens to Dahlonega, and the coaches wound in and out among the trees. The road in front of our house was higher than the yard. Father had let Mother choose between the Ben Hill house and the Thomas house, and she chose the latter.

"That was where we were reared. You can imagine what life around six boys would be like. One of Mother's best friends, a fine woman, taught a private school in a building erected for that purpose in her yard. That old house is still standing in the yard of that family's home. When it came time for us to enter school, Mother's friend told her that she simply couldn't have the six of us, for we were so noisy we would ruin her school.

"Well, that didn't keep us from going to school. Father just built a large, one-room building on the side of our yard and hired Professor Hudson as tutor. He and Father had been in the same company in the Civil War, and so Father knew him well and was satisfied that he was quite capable of teaching six noisy boys.

"It wasn't long before there were so many parents anxious to send their children to our school that Father put a partition in our schoolhouse and employed another teacher. He was Professor Orr from Martin Institute. Declamation time, as we called it then, was on Friday afternoons, and we invited our parents to attend and hear our speeches.

"At the closing exercises in June, Professor Hudson awarded a gold medal to the pupil who had maintained the best average throughout the school year.

"Well, instead of us breaking up the other school with our noise, it broke up because all its pupils came over to our school. Mother's friend was a wonderful teacher and a fine person in every respect, and we never had the least idea of making any trouble for her.

"My father was one of the instigators of the public school system in Athens. The first public school was on Meigs Street, and when that old building was torn down in later years, two houses were built from its timbers.

"Father was a great one for raising Jersey cattle, and gave each of us boys a male calf. We rode those calves all over town and probably would have ridden them to Sunday School, but mother wouldn't allow that.

"As far as you could see back of our house was in woods, and in the branch about where Boulevard now is, was 'the old swimming hole.' We boys went there every day in summer to swim. Bathing suits were unheard of.

"We just pulled off our brown-check pants and blue-check blouses and dove in. Every boy in town learned to swim in that old swimming hole. There was another one on the old Phinizy branch that we loved to swim in, too.

"Speaking of clothes, everybody wore cotton checks made in the old Check Mill, in summer. Even my father wore them. However, he had handsome broadcloth suits that he bought on his trips to New York. Winter clothes were of jeans, wool and cotton mixed, and this jeans material was manufactured in the same old Check Mill.

"Those were happy, carefree days for children. Every need was taken care of, but children didn't have money to waste like they do now, no matter how much their parents had.

"Dan was the name of one of Grandfather's slaves. When he was about eleven years old, he accidentally fell into the mill-race at Grandfather's cotton factory, and his head was so badly mashed that it never grew back into the right shape. When he got old enough to work, he became Grandfather's coachman.

"His wife was named Martha, and every Saturday all six of us boys would go out to their house for dinner. Such feasts as Dan and Martha did set before us—fried chicken, ham, and ash cakes, all cooked in an open fireplace, and if you have never eaten ash cakes you have missed the treat of your life.

"Grandfather was one of the first to have an interest in gold mining at Dahlonega. It was a two-day trip from Athens to Dahlonega then, and Grandfather made it about twice each year to see after his interests there.

"His oldest son was up there in charge of the work. When time came to go, two horses were hitched to a spring wagon that was loaded with trunks filled with bedding and food, and a trusted servant was sent on with it a day ahead of the family.

"He spent the first night at Jefferson, a distance of about twenty miles, and the second night he was scheduled to be in Sugar Hill. For a week before these trips, the coachman was busy shining up the carriage and all the silver on the harness. The family left in the carriage the day after the wagon set out, and usually overtook it at Sugar Hill.

"Some years ago I took Mother to Dahlonega for a day. I

picked her up at nine o'clock in the morning, then stopped by home for my wife and daughter. We arrived at our destination about noon. At three o'clock that same afternoon I told mother to get ready, as we were leaving for home.

"'Why George, you must be out of your mind,' she argued. 'You know this a two-day trip.'

"Anyway, we're leaving at three o'clock," I told her. "When we were back in Athens and she got out of my car at her home, the sun was still shining. Turning to me, she said: 'Well, I never thought I'd live to see the day when I could go to Dahlonega and back in one day.'

"One of Grandfather's sons followed in his footsteps as a builder. He was one of the three commissioners in charge of the construction of the State Capitol in Atlanta. Did you know that's the only State Capitol in the United States that was built within its appropriation?

"When that building was completed and all accounts paid up, there was a balance of $3.60 left.

"I believe I've already told you of some of our boyish pranks. What the six of us couldn't think of wasn't worth thinking of. We used to blacken thick ropes and pull them snake-like across the paths in front of courting couples that passed our yard at night. Our thick shrubbery made a grand hiding place for us to crouch in while we manipulated the strings that made the 'snakes' look more life-like.

"Once we stuffed a long black stocking and pulled it across the path in front of a young Hebrew couple and frightened them out of their wits. You could have heard them yell blocks away. Our parents heard the noise and stopped our fun when they learned that we were causing the racket.

"Dr. Billups was a fine old dentist practicing at Watkinsville. After his death, father bought his dental kit and gave it to me. The mahogany case was well equipped for that day and time, and I was just the proudest boy you ever saw. One day I was sitting on our front steps looking through the dental case when a neighbor came by.

"'Good morning, son! What are you doing?' he asked. "Waiting for a patient," I told him, as I held up the dental case.

"'Good!' he exclaimed, 'Come on down to my house and see what's wrong with this tooth that's hurting so bad right now.'

"When we arrived at his house, I had him seated in a chair, and in an exaggerated professional style, I took a piece of cotton from the kit, saturated it with oil of cloves and put it in the hollow of the aching tooth.

"My patient said it stopped the tooth from hurting and he paid me a nickel. That was the first money I ever earned, and from that time on the boys called me 'Doc.'

"The height of my ambition as a boy was to carry water on my head like our old cook, Cindy. 'Way back of our house, near the spring, we had a well dug that was sixty-two feet deep, and every morning Mother sent all six of us down there with Cindy and John, the gardener, for water. I tried and tried to carry a pail of water on my head, but was never able to accomplish this feat.

"We boys played many a day with the old ram that Mrs. Franklin had installed to pump water into her house. Here were the first waterworks we had ever seen. She had a slave that did nothing else but stand at that old ram all day and pump the water through the lead pipes to her house and gardens. During the war she had those old lead pipes taken up to be made into bullets for the soldiers.

"That old house has been changed quite a bit since then. At that time the entrance was on the west side of the house. There was even a *port-cochere* for the carriages to drive under. Three rooms extended across the front of the house, and now the entrance is in the middle room. The front porch has been added since then. Her porch was on the west side and its columns attracted lots of attention. They were put up just as the trees were when they were cut down—that is, the bark and stubs of the branches were still on them. One of the largest trees I have ever seen was in her back yard. All six of us boys used to clasp hands and try to reach around it, but our six pairs of arms were not long enough to encircle it.

"The interior of Mrs. Franklin's old house has been changed but little.

"Once when mother sent me to the dry well for something she needed, it was raining and the house girl had to go along with me to carry a lamp so I could see how to get around in that dark place. That was long before we had electric lights. I had to carry an umbrella to keep the rain from putting out the lamp.

"When we got back to the house, I was lowering the umbrella out on the back porch and got it caught in the lamp, which fell to the floor and exploded. The maid saw me through the flames and began yelling, 'Lord, have mercy! Marse Doc done burnt up. He's done daid!'

"She fainted dead away, and was taken to the servants' house. I wasn't hurt, but I was plenty scared. Father appeared and extinguished the fire by turning over a churn of milk on it. All through the night the poor house girl kept wailing, 'Lord, have mercy! I done killed Marse Doc.' Early the next morning I had to go down there and show her that I was alive and all right.

"I have in my possession now some of the old mantel paper made in the old paper mill. My uncle married the daughter of one of the owners of the paper mill. During the Civil war, this mill made the paper that was used for the wads to hold the powder in the guns. These wads were about four inches long and were twisted at both ends. The soldiers hastily bit off one end and rammed the wad into the barrel of the gun with the ramrod. The women made those wads at home. That was just one of the many ways they found to help out during the war.

"Quantities of rags were necessary for the manufacture of the paper, and people around here saved almost every scrap of fabrics to sell as rags at the paper mill. Rags finally became such a medium of local exchange that while those who preferred were usually paid in cash, others traded their rags for food or clothing, whichever they needed most.

"My college days were full of excitement, as well as hard work. I graduated from the University of Georgia in 1896 in Civil Engineering, and in 1897 in Electrical Engineering. I was the only one in my class to graduate in the latter subject. Henry Grady, Jr., [the son (?) of the Atlanta newspaper editor and exponent of "The New South"] was one of my schoolmates during the college days. He was a fine boy.

"In 1896 after Roentgen discovered the X-Ray, we made the first X-Ray picture ever made in the South in our classroom at the university, under Professor Patterson. That same year we also made equipment for sending wireless telegraphy at the university.

"When I left college in 1896, I went in business for myself. I think the little electric shop that I originated then was perhaps one of the first ever opened in Athens.

"Did I tell you that my Civil Engineering course was under Dr. Strahan? He was civil engineer for the county at the time, as well as an instructor at the university. He had charge of supervising the country roads as far back as the pick-and-shovel days. Those were the days when every property owner was called on to meet on a certain date to work the roads going through their own property.

"Dr. Strahan was instrumental in introducing plans for having the public roads worked at the expense of state and county. It was while he was on a trip to Europe and I was acting as County Engineer pro-tem in his absence, that the ruling [about state and county road expenses] went into effect.

"I sold my business here and entered business in Atlanta. That proved a failure. I returned to Athens and with one or two of my brothers and a few others, helped to put up a machine for making cement blocks, and we also installed a rock crusher. These blocks we made were the kind used in building houses.

"One or two of the houses made of our blocks are still standing here, and there are several elsewhere. I guess we were too far ahead of the times with that enterprise, so we gave it up.

"Work with the Bell Telephone Company drew me back to Atlanta. I have helped to run telephone lines from New Orleans to New York. I was working for them when the first underground cables, or wires, were laid from New York to Philadelphia, and when the tube was laid under the Hudson River.

"I was receiving an excellent salary and wouldn't have given up that work but for the fact that I was taken critically ill while in New York. As soon as I recovered sufficiently to make the trip, my wife and I returned to Athens to live. Soon after our return our daughter was born. She is our only child.

"As I told you, I had been sending my savings to my brother here to invest in real estate for me. I have always been interested in real estate, and I guess I've been active in the business for at least forty years.

"Getting to my experiences in this business of renting: we have some amusing as well as trying, experiences with Negro tenants. One of our houses has two large rooms and two small ones. A Negro man, his wife and five or six children lived in two of the rooms; a man and his wife occupied the other large room, and a girl rented the remaining small room.

"The girl hadn't paid her rent in three months. Every time Miss

Mamie went there to collect the rent, she was always told the girl was out. She never could find her in, so one night I took it upon myself to catch her in. I went there and found three Negro women sitting in that one little room. When I asked for the girl, they insisted, 'We don't know where she is. She ain't been here all day.'

"When I came home and told Miss Mamie, she said, 'Why George, you should have known better. Why didn't you try some other scheme to find out which one she was, instead of just asking them?'

"That's just one of the tricks that have been played on us. A white family was living in one of our houses, and whenever we went to collect the rent the man always had some excuse for not paying it. We were forced to take steps toward making him move out, so we gave him sixty days' notice. Still he didn't get out.

We issued a warrant, and he was to move by a stipulated date or the bailiff would clear the house. A man who said he was from out of town came to me for a house, so we rented him that one. In the lease it was plainly stated that he was to move in after the other family moved out. He said that he told the man who was living in the house that he was ready to move in and that he had already paid me some rent in advance.

"One day when he called on me, I asked him if the other family had moved out. He informed me they had not, but that he had moved in with them. I showed him the clause in his lease that read: 'You are to move in only when the other family now occupying the house has moved out.' I went straight to the bailiff. 'I'm paying you to do this work,' I reminded him. 'Why don't you do something about that warrant?'

"He went out to the house and put the furniture out in the yard. When I learned where he had placed it, I told him that would not do, for no one could move in the house as long as the furniture stayed on the premises. Then the bailiff moved it on the right-of-way across the railroad tracks. The railroad agent ordered me to move the goods from their property, for the owners of the furniture could sue the railroad company if a train came along and set fire to it. So the bailiff finally put the furniture in the street, as he should have done in the first place.

"It sat until the last piece had rotted down or was stolen. The owner never moved a piece of it. The funny part about the whole business was that the man who came here to rent the house was a brother of the woman who already lived there, and he was living there with them when be first came to see me about renting the house.

"They thought that by his making a new lease and paying the current rent they wouldn't have to pay up the back rent, or get out, either. Well, they couldn't pull that stunt on us.

"An apartment in the house back of our home here was rented to a couple. The woman was an artist and the son had what seemed to be a good job. They got about three months in arrears with their rent. When we felt that we had kept them as long as we could, we asked them to move. Often when we went to their apartment, we saw that they had much better food then we did. The woman put up an awful pitiful story in which she told us that her friends had sent in the food.

I found out that a missionary society in one of the local churches was feeding this couple. When a woman from this society called me to inquire about their financial troubles, I told her that I believed they were making enough to take care of their own expenses, and I couldn't understand why they were in such a jam.

She asked if we would be willing to pay the expenses of moving them. Now, I was glad to spend, say two dollars, to get them out, so I could rent the apartment to someone who would pay.

"I was surprised when the women from the missionary society

sent a large van to move them, for they were living in one of our furnished apartments and they only had about three or four suitcases and a few personal things. The bill rendered to me for the use of that moving van was $18. We investigated, and found they moved to Anderson, South Carolina, after we had been given the impression we were to pay for moving them to another apartment in Athens.

"All of our downtown store buildings are located in the best part of the business section, and we don't have to take any foolishness from the tenants. If they complain about the rent, all they have to do is move on out. We never have any trouble keeping those stores rented. Several of the tenants in those stores have been with us 25 years.

"However, we do have several small stores scattered over town that are hard to keep occupied. At the present time we don't have a single building, store, or residence, vacant. I don't think that's bad for 67 pieces of property to be kept rented.

"I'm not trying to give the impression that we own all of this property. We only have an interest in some of the buildings, and for various parcels of it I am administrator, agent, or guardian. Others of the parcels are our own individual property. We only have one-fifth interest in some of the property, for which I act as renting agent.

"We haven't followed the up-and-down trends of rental charges throughout the years. Our charge for Negro houses averages fifty [cents] a room per week, plus the water bill which amounts to about ten [cents] per room each week.

"We are subject to call, night or day. During the worst of the storm yesterday I had to go to a building that had sprung a leak in the roof. I would not delay, for after the rain ceased I wouldn't have been able to locate the leak. Some property owners have their repairs done only when they can't keep tenants any other way, but we try to keep up our repairs as we go along, just as fast as we can after learning of the need."

His eyes twinkled and he said: "In one of my apartment houses there are three families that I believe must take turns about staying awake at night to think up things they can ask me to do. You can't please some people, no matter how hard you try.

"Our rental prices range from two dollars to one hundred dollars per month. Five store spaces in one building rent for ninety-five dollars a month each. On some of the property the taxes and insurance run so high that we can hardly realize any profit from the rents.

"People from all walks of life will beat you if they can. You have to be on your guard at all times. A woman who was living in one of our houses went one night to call on an acquaintance across the railroad tracks. On the way back home she fell and skinned her leg. She sued us, telling the lawyer that her injury was incurred in a fall through a broken plank in the house she was renting from us. She had broken a plank in the kitchen to prove her point. Of course, we made her move. She lost the case.

"We only send the bailiff with a dispossessory warrant, as a last resort.

"My sister-in-law said to me one day, 'George, there's a family in one of my houses that I haven't heard from in some time. Will you find out what's the trouble?' I suggested that perhaps she had better go herself and investigate.

"She found that family in an awful condition. The man was drinking up everything he made and letting his family suffer. My sister-in-law went to the stores and bought what food and clothing they needed and carried it back to that poor woman and her children.

"This went on for a year—providing not only the rent, but their food and clothing as well. Finally we did succeed in getting

Interior of the Ross Crane house.
Photo credit: Historic American Buildings Survey

them out, but before they moved that man had the audacity to ask me to let then move in another of our houses that was vacant at the time.

"'Not a chance in the world,' I told him, 'What do you take me for?'

"Don't think for a minute that all our tenants are like the ones I have pictured to you. They are not, by any means. The renting game is like a mincemeat pie," he said with a twinkle in his eye, "for it's either good or bad. We complain about our piece of bad pie, but there's really not enough said about the good ones who pay their rent promptly and don't complain about this or that all the time.

"A professor and his family lived in one of our houses for eighteen months before I ever saw him or contacted him in any way, except that as regular as the second day of the mouth came around, his check came to us through the mails.

"We make it a point never to rent to undesirable people if we can help it. We investigate the character of the prospective tenant before the lease is signed, but even then we get bit some times.

"In one of our apartments last year, there was a person whose uncle was awfully attentive to her. We were suspicious of the two without a definite reason, so when this woman decided to move before the lease expired, we were delighted to see them go pleasantly and without hard feelings.

"Now, please don't misunderstand us. We are not as hardboiled as some of these things I've been telling you might picture us. We help our tenants just as much as we can, but after all, we didn't go into this game just because we love it.

"The business of renting was thrust upon us. We couldn't get an agent to look after it to suit us, so we decided to take it in charge ourselves. There's not enough volume in our rents to warrant maintaining an office downtown and to hire a secretary to do the typing and book-keeping, so we do the work ourselves right here in our own dining room at home.

"Yes, indeed, we rent to lots of mighty fine people and Miss Mamie and I enjoy having every one of them. We are proud of having that class of tenants.

"As to renting property; we live with it, eat with it at this very dining table, and we sleep and dream about it. We sleep four hours and work with our property the other twenty 'most every day. That's the life of people who rent real estate," he said.

Mrs. Lelia Bramblett

Editor's Note: Mrs. Lelia Bramblett lived at 157 Chattooga Ave., across the railroad track from the Southern Textile Mill, at the time of her interview on June 17, 1938. Mrs. Sadie Hornsby interviewed Mrs. Bramblett. No editor is listed. In the 1938 Athens City Directory she is listed as "Leila" Bramblett, wife of Henry T. Bramblett, owner of the Bramblett Barber Shop. Earlier, the Brambletts had lived at 480 Nacoochee, a few blocks from the Chattooga Avenue home. In the 1920 federal census, Mrs. Bramblett's name is given as"Leilia." Mrs. Bramblett died Jan 16, 1954. She was 76.

   The Bramblett's Chattooga house was in good condition in 2001, as was Henry Bramblett's restored, frame barbershop adjacent to the house.

• • •

When I arrived at Mrs. Bramblett's, she wasn't home. I rapped on the door, but there was no response. I rapped again and a vivacious young girl of high school age made her appearance from an adjoining room, which at one time had served as a barber shop.

"Are you looking for grandmother?"

I told her I was.

"Well, just come in and sit down. I am sure she will be here in a minute. She is always gone some place doing something for somebody. My name is Martha Jane Brown. I am her granddaughter."

I was invited into the living room. It was nicely furnished with modern furniture. In a few minutes Mrs. Bramblett came in, all out of breath.

She is a stout person, and was wearing a print dress, black shoes and gray hose. Her hair is gray, plaited in two long braids, wound around her head. She adjusted her silver-rimmed glasses as she came into the room.

She has a cute air about her. When she wants to make a statement she winks her right eye, nods her head and says: "Thar you are, huh?"

I got up when she entered the room. She laughed and began: "Well I be swear you did come, didn't you? Now just keep your chair—'taint no need to git up. Let me git a dip of snuff and I'll be with you.

"Now, lady, if you don't like my snuff, you needn't bother long or bother me because I am going to dip my snuff. And when I dip, I got to spit, even if the President of the United States was here.

"So you want me to tell you my life history? Well, if I told you all I know it would be a long one, but I don't know nothing so interesting. To tell the truth, I have been through so much and so many things have happened in the sixty-one year I have been here I have forgot what I did know.

"Ain't you cold? If you ain't, you look like it—all humped over that writing.

"I wish I could write—I can do right well at reading. Let me see how you spell my name.

"No, that ain't right. It's spelled with two 'Ts.' A heap of folks spells it with one, though.

"I was born and raised out at Princeton Factory. My mother didn't work in the mill after she married. She kept house, but Pa did. He made a dollar a day—he ran a picker machine.

Do you know what a picker machine is? Well, you tear a bale

of cotton up and put it in the picker. It chews and cuts that cotton all to pieces. From that room it went to the carding room, then to the spinners, on to the weaving room whar it was made into cloth.

"There warn't but two of us chillun—me and my brother. He didn't work in the mill till he was grown. My Ma and Pa moved to Winder, Georgy, after the Princeton Factory closed, and my brother went to work there as a weaver. Ma and Pa didn't stay in Winder not more than a year.

"They moved back here, and he worked in the Southern Mill. My brother went away out to Arkansas and was out there when my mother died. I ain't never seed him since. Fer all I know he is dead.

"When Ma died, Pa come to live with us. He died at my house.

"The Lord I pray, I went to work when I was ten year old. I went to school and my blame old teacher tried to make me write with my right hand, and I was left-handed. It messed my writing up, so I jes' quit fooling with 'em and went to work in the mill. I worked in the carding room and didn't make but thirty cents a day—that was considered big money fer a kid to make in them days, and chillun went to work by the time they was knee-high to a grasshopper.

"Now a carding machine is a great big machine you feed the cotton to, and it comes out in a great big old lap.

"When I was a little girl, Ma and Pa moved out to Whitehall to work in the mill for old man John R. White. He [Pa] done the same thing at Whitehall, he done at Princeton—he was a picker. We lived in a two-room log cabin. We lived in one room and cooked and ate in the other. We lived out there about six months.

"The house we lived in at Princeton was a nice house for that time. There was two rooms on the first floor and one upstairs. They were large rooms, and all the houses were ceiled like this one of mine is.

"When I was little, I was crazy about brown sugar. Did you ever see any? We kept it by the barrel at our house, but to me it warn't nigh as good as Mrs. Ridley's, who lived a little way up the road. I used to take my little tin cup and go to her house every morning for brown sugar. It was the best stuff I ever tasted.

"I never will forget one morning, well, I set out with my cup to Mrs. Ridley's. When I got in sight of her house, I seed a man sitting on her porch. That was the funniest thing to me because I had never seed a man at her house before, because she was a widow woman and it wasn't nobody lived thar but she and her daughter, Willie.

"When I seed that man, I tucked my little tail and started back home, as fast as I could go. She called me back, but I didn't pay her no mind. When I got home, Ma asked me, 'What's the matter? Didn't you get no sugar?' I told her the trouble and she said, 'tain't nobody but her brother.'

"I went on back and got my sugar.

"Not long after that we moved back to Princeton, and I sure did miss Mrs. Ridley. One day I happened to go to Mrs. McLerey's. She give me a tea cake.

"Back in them days all the houses had paling fence around them. Mrs. McLerey lived right back of our house. It was too much trouble to go all the way around, so I tore a paling off the back fence, and every day I would slip through and go to her house for my tea cakes. I thought she had the prettiest white table cloth I ever saw.

"Mr. Henry Lovern was the boss, and his brother, Mr. Horace Fred, was the Super [supervisor] over the carding room. They were good bosses. They looked after the welfare of their hands, and saw to it that the houses were in good condition and fitten to live in. The size of the house depended on the size of the family you had. If your family was small, you had a small one. A big family got a larger house.

"We rented the houses from the mill, and when you got your pay ticket, the rent was took out of your pay."

She laughed and said: "I am here to tell you the boss was my sweetheart. I went with him till he married; me and his sister run together. The reason I didn't marry him was I didn't want him. He married Beckey Dye.

"If this here story I am telling you ever comes out in a book— course I ain't expecting it to—but if it does—I sure hope Henry gets holt of it and reads it if he is living, and as fer as I know he is.

"Do you know, he fixed up his house and bought every stitch of the furniture before he was married? He come by my house the day before he married and took me to see his new home. He told me if I would marry him that day, the house would be mine.

"I told him. 'No, it won't, neither.'

"He was a heap older than I was—me and him jes' claimed each other as sweethearts. I use to get a heap of fun making the girls mad taking their beaus away for them.

"I don't recollect nary one of my grandparents on my mammy's side. My grandfather worked in Princeton mill. I don't know if my grandmother worked or not. I heard my Ma say she [the grandmother] was an Irishwoman and come to this country when she was sixteen year old. They said she was a little bitty woman. They lived in Madison County before they moved to Athens.

My mother was a Stephens before she married. When my grandmother and grandfather died, my mother was just a little girl. There were four girls and two boys. The oldest went to work in the mill and raised the least ones. The oldest were about grown when they come to Princeton. They were weavers and made fifty cents a day. They got twelve-and-a-half cents a cut, and they got about four cuts a day, which amounted to fifty cents.

"You know my chillun calls me old fashion because I don't try

The Bramblett barber shop and house, 157 Chattooga Ave.
Taken in 2001. *Photo credit:* Al Hester

to dress like they do and talk proper. I don't care none. I tells them I can make rings around them now when it comes to doing things. Why, do you know when I was a young girl they used to wear drawers and call them bloomers. We wore long dresses and cotton stockings.

"I can't say that the health conditions in mills were any different back then from what they are now. Of course, there warn't no hospitals nor health clinics. When the hands got sick, the doctors warn't up on their profession like they are now, and the hands went on and died like Henry's [Henry Bramblett] first wife.

"She couldn't give birth to her child, so she died.

"She was sixteen year old to the day when she died. She had been married exactly one year. She worked in the mill before she married Henry—she was a spinner.

"I told you I stopped school because they wanted me to write with my right hand. We didn't have a school house at Princeton.

The Methodist church was used as a school. Back in them days thar warn't no such thing as free schools. You had to pay a dollar a head for every kid in school—that money went for the teacher's salary. Miss Jemantha Ward was my first teacher.

"Henry's father, Mr. Bramblett, was my next teacher, and Miss Barton was the last teacher I had. She taught in a little one-room shack. Yes, Miss Barton tried to make me write with my right hand, and I was as left-handed as a jack rabbit.

"Most of my teachers were women. They didn't skeer me.

"When Old Man Bramblett made his appearance, I would begin to cry—I was afraid of that man as a bear.

"Then the Stypher Smith boys come to Princeton to put up a night school. They taught penmanship. I went one night—they wouldn't let me use my left hand, so I didn't go back.

"I ain't ashamed of my reading, but when it comes to writing, about all I can do is write my name.

"The company had a store. Once a week the hands went to the store and got their supply of rations, and it was taken out of their pay ticket. We were paid off once every four weeks. It didn't take much to live on back then. Eggs were ten cents a dozen, butter ten cents a pound, milk five cents a gallon, fat-back sold for four and five cents a pound, and chickens ten or fifteen cents apiece.

"Flour was mighty cheap, too.

"People lived at home them days. Ma had her own cow, hogs, chickens and garden. They didn't know what conveniences were—it was jes' like living in the country sure enough. Didn't have no such thing as restrictions, such as how close the hog pen was to the house, and water works were unheard of.

"I am sixty-one year old, and I have never been out of Georgy but once in my life. My daughter was living in South Carolina. They sent me word to come at once—she was dying. I hustled to see her. She lived jes' a few hours after I got to her house.

I brought her chillun home with me and raised them—they are grown and married now. When I was on the train going to see my daughter, when I saw them electric lights, I didn't act like 'Aunt Nancy and Uncle Josh,' a record we used to have on the graphyphone.

"I am sorry them old things went out of style. I liked to play the records—I jes' despise a radio."

Her daughter Virginia came to the door and announced supper was ready. Mrs. Bramblett looked at the clock.

"Well, I'll be, I have been talking the blessed afternoon and you haven't finished yet. I know you are tired and I sure am."

I asked if I might return early the next morning:

"Sure, sure I want you to," she said.

• • •

When I reached her house early the next morning, she was in her bedroom. It was in perfect order. On the bed was a green frog pillow, and a tabby cat was snuggled close to the pillow.

"Have a chair and take off your hat and coat—let them dry while you are talking," Mrs. Bramblett said.

"Let me see, I left off yesterday where I went to see my daughter in South Carolina."

"After Henry's wife died, he went three year before he ever spoke to me. I ran into him one day in the mill. We started to going together regular after that. We met at his father's house to do our courting. We ran away and married.

"I was born on the first day of February one minute past twelve o'clock, 1878. My Ma said I was walking and talking since I was nine months old and have been talking every since.

"I worked in the mill for six months after I married. I reckon you know the rest.

"When I was a little thing, they said I was never still five minutes. Saint Lovern told me if I would sit still five minutes he would give me a nickel. I sat still, but he never give me that nickel.

"A long time after I had been married, he come back to visit his brother. His brother said to me, 'Lelia, do you know who this is?'

"I said, 'No, who is it?'

"'It is Saint Lovern,' he said.

"'Gimme that nickel you promised me,' I said. He laughed and laughed, 'Why, Lelia, haven't you ever forgotten that?'

"I told him 'No, and I never would.'

"I called him my sweetheart when I was a little girl. He was a sight older than me. I used to watch for him going to work, and when I saw him coming I would hop up on the gate-post. He come by, would kiss me and keep going.

"We lived at Princeton ten years after we married. Three of my children was born there and three over here at the Southern Mill. When they were large enough to work, all of them worked in this mill down here as weavers. The cloth they made was coarse, white cloth. I don't know what it was used for, as all of it was shipped to a northern market for sale.

"When Princeton mill shut down, then we moved to the Southern Mill and have been here every since. Yes, we have been living here thirty-one year. When Henry went to work in this mill, he done the same kind of work, only he made a dollar a day.

"In my young days we used to get together on Saturday nights and have our little parties. The older folks danced and the younger ones jes' frolicked and had a fine time. Bless your life, we had better be in by nine o'clock, or our parents would be out looking for us to find out the reason why.

"I never will forget one weekend Pa and Ma went out in the country to spend the night. My Ma had taken an orphan girl into our home to raise.

"She and Ruth, my cousin, and me decided to have a 'dumb

The abandoned Southern Textile Mill where Brambletts worked.
Taken in 2001. *Photo credit:* Al Hester

supper.' Did you ever hear of one? We done every thing back'ards.
I don't remember jes' what we had to eat—nothing but bread and
meat, I believe. Anyway, we didn't speak a word while we were
having it. It's a wonder I didn't. I was such a talker, the girls didn't
like me much because I would tell on them.

"About eight o'clock Henry come in the back door. We had the
table all ready fixed when they got there. We girls were sitting by
the fireplace in the kitchen and hadn't spoke a word since we
started. I don't know why they went in the back door unless they
saw a light in the kitchen.

"They must have known what was going on because they
didn't say a word.

"Henry sat down in Ruth's chair first, then changed and sat
down in my chair. Me and Ruth set our plates on the backside of
the table; Emma fixed hers on the front side.

"She and Jim married, and he later become a Baptist preacher. Henry and Jim didn't say a word when they come in and sat down, but I did. I asked them what they come fer. I didn't like Henry then, so I run them home. Henry married Ruth, my first cousin.

"She lived a year. Three year later, we married.

"In those days, hoop dresses and bustles were a mighty go. I was married in a dove-colored dress trimmed in dove-colored ribbon. I say silk. We didn't know what a silk dress was, they were for the rich. I remember a girl I ran with was going to get married, and we decided to borrow the dresses from two girls who had just married.

"We asked them to lend us their dresses. They said, 'all right, but what are you going to do with them?'

"I wouldn't tell 'em. They lent us everything they were married in—dresses, undercoats, drawers, shoes, stockings, even to their hats and gloves.

"Nettie, the girl getting married, said it would bring her good luck, if I didn't tell what I borrowed 'em for. The next day I marched down to the Justice of the Peace with her to get married. On the way I had a fuss with the boy I was to stand up with. We were already on the outs with each other a little bit anyhow, so when we got there I wouldn't stand up with him.

"There was a right smart difference in the way things were run in the Southern Mill than at Princeton Factory. For one thing they had more to do with over here [at Princeton]. When we first moved to this place there wan't a store, church and a mighty few houses on this hill. We had to go way over on Prince Avenue to buy our rations—we bought enough to last two weeks. Rations warn't nigh as high as they are now.

"Every now and then the mill would build a new house. I have seen them go up and now they are going down.

"Away back yonder when any of the hands got sick, the bosses were mighty good about letting them have money and pay it back when they went back to work. When one of the hands died and the family warn't able to bury them, the boss let the family have money and pay it back when they could."

A man in work clothes stuck his head in the door.

"Good morning, where is Gin?"

"She has gone to take Naomi to nursery school," Mrs. Bramblett answered. "Look here—make your self useful and make a fire in the stove. It is most nigh time for Gin to cook dinner."

He went to the kitchen, and there were sounds of the fire being made. In a short while Gin, Mrs. Bramblett's daughter, came in.

She, like her mother, weighs nearly 200 pounds. She was wearing a print dress, black sweater and shoes without hose. She took off her coat and shook the rain from it. Filling her mouth with snuff, she asked, "Mama, did you give the lady some of the candy I made yesterday?"

"No, bring us some. It is powerful hard, but it sure tastes good."

Gin left the room, returning with a huge piece of white sugar candy in her hand, the size of a goose egg, and gave it to me.

I offered it to Mrs. Bramblett .

"You break it," she said. "I don't want to put my hands on it before you, because I don't know what these sores on my hands might be. Gin, you better git to work on that dinner. What are you going to cook—some pinto beans?'

"No," said Gin. "I bought a bunch of the prettiest collards at the store you ever seen. I think I will cook them and some dried butter beans."

She soon left the room.

"Yes, we are living in a new day now, about twenty-five year ago we organized a club in the community called the 'Lend a Hand Club.' The object of it is to help them that can't help themselves. We look after the sick, buy coal, food, clothing and buy medicine. The way we make our money is by having suppers, quiltings and selling the quilts.

"We are planning to have a minstrel at the Community House tonight. The admission is ten and twenty cents, a very liberal price. Jess Baxter is putting it on, and every blooming time he comes here, it rains. He brings his own cast; we don't have enough young folks in this community that has talent enough to put on a dog fight.

"The Community House use to be the school. It was first put up for the village, but when this side of town begun to build up, the chillun come over here to school. There were soon too many for the school and Chase Street School was built. Now the old school is used as a gathering place for the village.

"The girls have a glee club conducted by Miss Lucile Crabtree.

"There were so many chillun on the streets and nothing to do, so I went to the authorities of the mill and arranged to have a playground at the Center. Now we have a nice nursery for the smaller ones from 9 to 11:30 in the morning and a playground for the older ones in the afternoon. They also have indoor games on bad days. This is sponsored by the WPA with capable leaders in charge.

"Miss Julian—I have forgotten her first name—started the 'Lend a Hand Club.' She lived over here on Hiawassee. She went to every woman in the village. Them what wanted to join and attend regular was put on one list, the ones who can't is put on another, called the honorary list. The dues are ten cents a month.

"Henry got tired of working the mill and decided to change jobs. That was a long time before the mill shut down. He worked on the police force awhile; then he opened a barber shop right out here by the side of the house and did a good business. After the mill closed, he moved it downtown, as there was not enough business in the village to keep it open. He has been downtown every since.

"We have been in this house for seventeen years. We bought it the day Jim, my boy, was sixteen.

"Once I went to the door, and there stood a darkey. He said, 'Miss, don't think anything about me standing here, but the last time I was along here, where this house stands was a cotton field. I have picked cotton and pulled corn through here many a day long before there was even a railroad run through this place. They used to have Holiness meetings across the railroad tracks.'

"One night I was going to meeting, and a boy was standing on the bridge that crossed the railroad. He helloed at me: 'Mrs. Bramblett, whar are you going?'

"I said, 'To the Holiness Meeting.' He said, 'To get happy?'

"I said, 'And stay all night.'

"And from that we got to calling it 'Happy Top.' It was kinder a rough place, too. After it started building up, all kinds of people started moving in, drinking and cutting up. They were kind-hearted in their way, but rough as could be.

"When the mill shut down, the folks had to leave and the houses have rotted down. You take that apartment house on Park Avenue, it was a nice building. Jes' one family after another lived in it. They didn't know how to take care of it—they soon tore it to pieces. I think the rooms rented for twenty-five cents each.

"That mill has never done no good since the war [World War I] and everything has gone up so. During the war I made thirty-five dollars a week. They don't pay no such salaries as that now."

A girl came in. She was wearing a gay print dress, a sweater over her head to keep off the rain, and a pair of knee-length boots completed her costume. She went over to the fire without an invitation, spitting a mouthful of snuff into the fire.

Turning to me she asked: "What are you doing—taking census?"

"No, we are in the movies. Don't you think I will make a good actress?"

The girl tried every way to find out what I was writing. Seeing that Mrs. Bramblett didn't want her to know [what we were doing] I let her do the talking.

After she saw it was no use trying to find out what I was writing, she remarked: 'Well I reckon my feet are dry enough—can I use your phone?"

"Yes, but you be sure you don't have any mud on your feet. If you mess up Martha Jane's room, she will bless you out."

When she left the room, Mrs. Bramblett said: "Ain't it funny how folks hang around to find out your business? I am glad you let me do the talking.

"Yes, Ma'am, times sure have changed terrible, back yonder from what they are now. Even in clothes it used to take five and ten yards of cloth to make a dress. Now you can get one out of three.

"The neighbors have changed, too. Everybody use to be neighborly, helping those that couldn't help themselves. Now they don't pay any attention whether they are starving, half clothed or sick. Don't mix and mingle, or swap jokes like they use to.

"We used to have to go to church or we didn't go no whar else. When I was a child I used to have to sit on the front seat. When the old women got to shouting, I had to crawl up on the bench to keep them off my toes.

"I never wore no shoes to church—all the little chillun went to church and Sunday School bare-footed.

"There were no such thing as free schools in my day, but I don't call them free now—heap more chillun would be in school around here if they didn't have to pay so much for the use of their books, pencils and paper as well as other things they use in school now. Chillun warn't made to go to school in my day. That is the reason I quit school and went to work.

"Do you know I have picked cotton many a day across that railroad where you see them houses. Back yonder, folks went to work in the mill by the time they was knee-high to a duck. Now they won't let 'em work till they are too old.

"When I lived at Princeton, there was an old darkey who come to my house every Sunday morning and cooked breakfast for us. When that coffee got to stinking in the kitchen, it made me some hungry.

"He called us his white chillun. When he left my house and went to cook dinner for my sister-in-law, I was right behind him. The other folks' cooking smells better than that you cook your self."

Virginia came to the door: "Mama, are you going after Naomi, or do you want me to go? Seems to me you ought to have told the woman everything you ever knew by this time."

"I could tell her a heap more if I didn't have to go to school for the baby, and its 11:30 now."

Mrs. Bramblett got up, put on a heavy black coat, and we started out in the rain for the little girl, and I on my way back to town. On the way she said: "You think these streets are bad now, but you ought to have seen them several year ago."

We turned into Chase Street, and she continued: "This street used to be a perfect loblolly before they paved it."

We reached the Community Center.

"Well, this is where we part. I sure have enjoyed your visit. Come back to see me and spend the day. If my story gets into print, I sure do want to buy one of them books," Mrs. Bramblett said.

The last I saw of her she was crossing the muddy street in the direction of the Community House.

Mariah Jackson

Editor's Note: Mrs. Mariah Jackson, midwife, was interviewed on Dec. 13, 1938, by Mrs. Grace McCune. Her address was given as 181 Lyndon Row, but in the 1938 city directory it is shown as 183 Lyndon Row, and no occupation is listed for her. Mariah Jackson said in her interview that she was 79 years old, born in Notasulga, Alabama.

The Athens Banner-Herald *on Dec. 21, 1938, carried the obituary of Mrs. Jackson, an unusual event, as she was black. She had died December 20, only a week after she was interviewed by Mrs. Grace McCune, who also went to her funeral and gives a detailed account of it at the end of the interview.*

• • •

A search for Mariah's abode led up and down Georgia's steep, red hills that in this particular section had been converted into slick, red mire by a downpour of rain. My frequent inquiry, "Can you direct me to Mariah Jackson's house?" invariably received this response, "It's just 'round the corner to your right."

But they failed to tell me how many corners were to be turned before I would finally arrive at the four-room house occupied by the old granny woman. Except for need of a coat of paint the dingy little structure seemed to be in good condition. The small yard space that led from the street to the narrow porch was clean-swept.

At one side was a large, grassy plot where a few late chrysanthemums were bravely trying to hold up their heads. Two doors confronted me as I entered the porch, and my knock on the first one was answered by a tall young Negro who said, "Mariah, she lives next door." As I extended my hand to rap on the adjoining door it was opened by a tiny boy, black and shiny, attired in clean, blue overalls and a red sweater.

"I heared you ask for Mariah; she's right here if you wants to see 'er."

A small mulatto woman came to the door. "I'se Mariah," she said. "Won't you come in and set down?"

Mariah led the way into a bedroom where a glowing laundry heater was a welcome sight after the long, cold, and very wet tramp in search of her house.

"I hope you will 'scuse the cookin'," said Mariah as she hastened to turn over a pone of cornbread that was smoking in its pan on the heater. Next to it a coffee pot was emitting a cloud of steam, and the remainder of the space on the small stove was occupied by a heavy iron frying pan covered with a close-fitting lid.

"I don't s'pect you likes this," she remarked as she removed the lid from the frying pan. "This is chit'lins. Some of my friends done kilt hogs and sent 'em to me, and if you don't mind, I'd like mighty well to finish cookin' our eats 'cause I'se hungry."

This last remark seemed a good cue for my presentation of the sack of fruit I had brought with me, and I urged her to proceed with her cooking.

Mariah was delighted. "Chile," she exclaimed. "I knows who you is now. You'se that white chile my Mr. Aaron said was comin' to see me. That man sho' knows how good old Mariah loves fruit, and I'll just bet he put you up to fetchin' it to me."

While Mariah was busy, I looked around the clean, comfortable and home-like room with its simple furnishings. Crinkled cotton spreads covered the mattresses on the two iron beds.

There was a beautiful fern on an old-fashioned washstand. Other furnishings included two trunks, several chairs and a small table or two. A small dog and a cat were sleeping near the stove.

The old-style chimney, built out into the room, had a mantel on which were several tins of wandering Jew and a large oil lamp. One corner of the room was curtained off with portieres made of flour sacks. The rough, wide planks that formed the walls were whitewashed.

A small girl, apparently not more than eight years old, was ironing on a board placed on two chairs.

"Stop your work, honey," Mariah addressed the child. "Git you semolina' to eat and eat it, and then go outside and play while we talks."

Turning to me, she said, "I tries to learn 'em how to work, 'cause I knows I'se going to be called away one of these days to come back here no more. Yes, Lord, that I is, that's a fact, honey, sho' as you'se borned."

When she had placed a piece of cornbread and a serving of chitterlings on each of their plates, she opened the sack of fruit and gave each child an apple and sent both of them to the kitchen to eat.

"I ain't going give 'em none of my oranges 'cause with just one tooth in my haid, I kin eat them better'n any of the other fruit."

When she had heaped her own platter with chitterlings and cornbread and had poured a cup of coffee, she sat down by me, near the stove, and soon was rocking in her chair, as she consumed her food with every indication of satisfaction. I wondered how she could attain such gusto with only one tooth. A widespread, checked apron almost covered her clean, dark print dress, and a little fringe of gray hair escaped the snowy head rag.

As she ate, she talked: "I'se sho' glad Mr. Aaron done sent you to see me," she said, "And I told Molly just last night that Mr.

Aaron hadn't never lied to me before. It had been such a long time since he had sent me word you was coming, that I'd done plum' give you out."

The platter had been sopped clean with the last of the cornbread, and she reached into the sack for an orange.

"Chile," she said. "I'se mighty proud and thankful you gimme this fruit. I was just a-wishin' this very mornin' that I had some."

The dog woke up and started around the heater to investigate the presence of a stranger.

"Don't let him touch your stockin's," said Mariah, "'Cause he'll tear 'em sho' as you'se borned. Course he don't aim to; he's just such a friendly little pup. We don't know who he belongs to. He just took up here and the chillun wanted 'im so bad, I just couldn't say 'no.'

"Our cat is right smart, too. I sho' don't never see no rats around here. "Now, if you don't mind, I'll put on a pot of peas to cook for the other chillun to eat when they gits home atter school.

"I'se awful slow about doin' things, 'cause I'se done got so old and no-count these days."

Soon after she had replenished the fire, and the peas had begun to boil, she placed a generous quantity of snuff in her mouth and settled back in her chair. Then we heard a knock at the door.

Mariah introduced the aged Negro woman who entered, as "Miss Jenny." Jenny used the next few moments to tell Mariah about her "job of work with some white folkses, what lives a fur piece off. The man's a-comin' atter me in a great big autymobile tomorrow."

Her story told, Jenny took her departure with the final remark, "I didn't know you all had no company, Miss Jackson—I'll run along now, and come back to see you another time."

After she was gone, my hostess chuckled.

"She just had to know who it was here to see me, and when you'se gone evvy blessed woman around here will trump up some 'scuse to come and try to find out what you wanted, but ain't none of 'em going to find out nothin' from Old Mariah."

Again Mariah started her story, "I don't 'spect I can tell you much about what you wants to know, 'cause my mind ain't so good as it used to be. Sometimes I can remember things way back yonder good, and then again my memory just comes and goes. I don't recollect much about the time before the war [Civil War], 'cause I was too young myself then, but I'se going to do my best to tell you the answer to anything you asks me.

"You want to know why? Hit's 'cause my boy, my Mr. Aaron, done sent you to see me.

"I was borned 79 years ago last March, away down in Alabamy at a place they called Notasulga. My Daddy had done been borned and raised on Dr. Crawford Long's place in Oglethorpe County, Georgy. Chile, Daddy's marster, Mr. Long, was such a grand, good man, they named a town in Oglethorpe County for him [Crawford]. His wife—she was Miss Annie May Long—was one good woman in this here world of sin and sorrow. All that Long family was good white folkses.

"Sam Foster was my Daddy, and he comed all the way to Alabamy to marry my Mammy, and he stayed on in Alabamy till long atter the big war was over. Mammy's name was Sue.

"She had been sold off one time in her life, but when she married, she belonged to Miss Grace Bradford. There was one child younger'n me, born durin' the war. It was a long time atter the war was over before our white folkses would tell Mammy and Daddy that we was free, and it was a longer time yet before we could come to Georgy.

"My granddaddy sent atter us. Yes, that he did. He sent one horse and wagon plum' to Alabamy to fetch us back. The man he

sent was sick with a swelling when he got to Alabamy; he was just
swelled up all over. I ain't never seed the like, and it was sho' a
mighty long time before he was able to ride back in that wagon.

"I don't know just how many days it took to come from
Alabamy to Oglethorpe County in Georgy, but Daddy said it was
sho' a long, hard trip. Roads warn't like they is now and folkses
lived a long piece apart. Semolina to eat was hard to git on the
road, and they was hungry plenty of times before they got to the
end of that long ride.

"Daddy and the boys rid in that wagon with the man what had
the swellin', but Mammy and us two gals ride the train. I ain't
never going to forgit comin' to Georgy, because that was my fust
train ride, and I was scared plum' to death.

"Mammy said I screamed and carried on so when that train
come puffin' up to the depot, she thought they never would be
able to git me on it. She said I held on to her all the time on the
train, till we got hungry and she opened up a big box of something to eat, what she had done cooked up before we left
Alabamy.

"Big as that box was, the eats give out on us long before we got
to granddaddy's house, and we was hungry sho' enough all the
last part of that long ride.

"Granddaddy's house was on the old Long place down on the
Georgia Railroad. Right there's the place I growed up in. I stayed
there till I married, workin' in the field with my Daddy, 'cause
that was all the kind of work I knowed how to do them days.

"They had schools, but there warn't none on our place. But
schoolin' warn't no fur piece off, 'cause there was a school in
Foster Town. That was a place what had so many Fosters livin' in
it that they sho enough did call it Foster Town. Lots of the young
chillun was sent to that school, but me, I ain't never went to no
schoolhouse a whole day in my borned days.

"I hear folkses talk about them A-B-C's, but I don't know nothin' about 'em. But just let me tell you, there sho' can't nobody fool me when it comes to countin'. I can sho' do that. There don't nobody beat Old Mariah out of nothin'.

"All of Daddy's chillun had to help him in the field. We worked mighty hard, but we had a good living; there was plenty to eat, a place to stay, and evvything we sho' enough needed.

"My Daddy seed to it that I had a mighty smart weddin', when me and Joe Jackson got married. It was just one of them old-time country weddin's. Daddy didn't invite so powerful many folks, but it was a nice weddin' right on.

"I don't even remember what color my dress was. It was made out of thin cloth that had light dots on it. It may of been dotted Swiss. I don't know.

"There was the mostest good things to eat at our weddin' supper. Daddy even had a whole hog cooked for us, but we wouldn't allow no dancin' round there. I minded my good old Daddy, and I ain't never danced one of them sets in my whole life, and at my age I don't never 'spect to. Even if I wanted to do it, I'se done got too stiff and no 'count.

"Even if Daddy hadn't minded, I ain't never had no time for dancin' nohow. I worked hard and tried to take care of what us made. Me and Joe farmed for white folkses for years and years. I worked right along with Joe in the field, 'cause I'se a-tellin' you he was a good man, through all the fifty years we lived together. He has been gone and left me eight years ago prezackly, since five o'clock last Friday evenin'.

"I don't remember how come I done it, but I got started in as a granny woman not long before we moved into town. That's been more'n thirty years ago. Since that time I'se been doing that kind of wuk all along. till I got too old and quit, about three years ago.

"Course you ain't supposin' to know much about my kind of work, but it's sho' enough hard work. Why, I'se cotched as many as three babies in one night. Chile, is you married, or is I a-tellin' you what I hadn't oughta?"

Considerable urging was necessary before Mariah was convinced that it was proper for an unmarried woman to hear her story.

"Atter I come here to town I worked with Miss Eckford and Miss Bryan. Course, I had to take them blood testies then, and wear white gowns, and I wore white caps that kivvered up all my hair. And does you know, they had to see me do some of my work before they would allow me to have one of them 'stificates. The funny part of it all is that I 'spects I was cotchin' babies before them womans was borned themselves.

"Miss Eckford, she was good and all right, but I just loved to work with Miss Bryan, and she still comes to see me about one time evvy week.

"Yas, Lord, I'se cotched plenty of babies as they comed into this old world. That I has, and Miss Bryan, she always said she didn't never worry about none of Mariah's cases, 'cause if there was anything wrong, Mariah would sho' say so.

"Plenty of folkses right in this very town still owes me for waitin' on 'em. Yas, Lord, there's plenty owin' to me that I don't never 'spect to git. Some folkses would pay if they could; others just ain't got no mind to pay me nothin'.

"Laugh? Why, I'se never seed nothin' to make me want to laugh at on none of my cases; them womans was always sufferin' too much for that. I'se heared other granny womans laugh about how their cases behaved, but it warn't like that with me. I always wanted to visit with my cases before they was down in the bed and sho' enough needed me.

"That was so I could be sho' evvything was fixed up ready, just so. But, yas, Lord, I'se fussed at 'em plenty of times, just to git 'em good and mad, that I has. It was for their own good, for if I could just git 'em mad enough, it was easier on 'em and was all over quicker.

"I'se seed plenty of sufferin' and sad times with the rich, the pore, the white, and the colored womans. Yas, Lord, that I has, for I'se worked with 'em all.

"My job was to cotch the babies, and see that evvything was all right before I left the place, and I always went back evvy day for seven days to see that they was gittin' along all right. If they was doing well on the seventh day my work was finished.

"But now, I'se got too nervous and old. You know, that's work that can't wait. I had to go right on when they called me, rain or shine, sleet or snow. That chile what opened the door when you come here, that's my great-great grandchile, and he's just about the last baby I cotched. Now, I did go out just this last week here in the neighborhood, but it was just to help Miss Bryan out, 'cause she is so nice and good to me.

"I'se had fourteen chillun myself, eight boys and six gals. Yas, Lord! Praise the Lord! I'se still got eight of my chillun left livin'. Most of 'em lives close by in this neighborhood, 'ceppin' one gal that lives in Cincinnati.

"I'se worked hard to raise my chillun and send 'em to school. Some of my oldest ones went to the country schools before we moved to town.

"Joe worked and I worked, and my white folkses has been mighty good to me. I just don't know what I would do if it warn't for 'em. Let me tell you, I sho' did have a good husband.

"He made fifteen dollars a week, working at the Holman Building, and evvy Saturday night he fetched evvy last penny of that money straight home and laid it in my lap. When I asked him how much he wanted out of it, he always said 'fifty cents.' And what do you think he wanted with them fifty cen'ses? Not a blessed thing but to buy my snuff with. That's right.

"I done housework and washin', too, for some of my good white folkses, and I took good care of what we made, so we would have something. Other folkses, they says, 'Miz Jackson, how does you git along so well? How come you has so much?'

"Us always had plenty somepin to eat, good clothes to wear, and a good home to live in. Them other folkses never worked like us done, and what they made, they never took no care of. I made our chillun work, too. Our white folkses said all my family was good workers. Since I'se got too old to work no more, them chillun of mine has been mighty good.

"Some of 'em's always sendin' something for me.

"We lived in one house for nigh on to thirty years, but it warn't here. I'se just been here 'bout one year. My gal what lives in Cincinnati, sent for me to come live with her. I got rid of almost all my things and went, but shucks, seven months was long as I could stay up there.

"I was too homesick, so she had to send me back. Callie got this place. We has two of the rooms, and one of my gals lives in the two rooms on the other side. She works out, and I takes care of her chillun whilst she's gone evvy day.

"All my chillun's been mighty good to me, but my Emma, she never would leave me to git married. Yas, Lord, that chile has sho' stayed with her old Mammy. They was all of 'em mighty good to me in Cincinnati, but I was scared I might die away off up there, and I wants to be laid in the ground right long side of Joe, and these chillun of ours had sho' better see to that.

"I believes in in-surance. That I does! I'se got a policy that will pay for puttin' me in the ground, when I'se called away from this world.

"I ain't never been to no doctor for myself and I ain't never had no doctor sent here. I don't take no medicine neither, but I knows a man what kind of fixes me up something when I feels like I needs it. That's sho' enough. The last time I had a bad hurtin', I just went to see him, and told him I had a hurtin' in my right side under my shoulder. He walked around me a time or two, and then he rubbed that side, and said, 'It's all right now.' And it was. It ain't hurt me no more since.

"I ain't sick now—I'se just no 'count. I'se gittin' old. I fell last week and hurt myself right bad. I couldn't git up, and if it hadn' a been for that little great-great grandson of mine, I 'spects I would have had to stay on the floor till Callie got home. But he called a lady in to help me git up.

"My laig's been a-hurtin' me right smart ever since.

"Does you know what time it is?" asked Mariah, as she stirred the pot of peas. I told her that according to my wrist watch it was 2:10. She sipped water from a dipper for a while, gave the restless dog some food, then sat down in her rocking chair and put it in motion again.

She seemed to be pondering something as she solemnly and silently studied my face. Finally she asked, "Is you kin to Miz Josie Stewart? You all sho' do favor. You'se just a-like."

I admitted that I was not related to Mrs. Stewart. Expecting to please her, I added that I knew Mrs. Stewart and admired her.

"I 'spects she's good,"answered Mariah. "I washed for her family for years.

"I sho' does like Mr. Gilbert Stewart. He is one good man. That he is! This here's his house. He lets me have these two rooms for a dollar a week, and he sometimes says, 'Mariah, don't you worry none if you don't have the rent right ready evvy time.' Now that's just like Mr. Gilbert Stewart."

Suddenly she stopped rocking and asked. "What day is this, anyhow?"

I told her it was Tuesday.

"I means, what day in the month is it?" When I replied that it was the 13th of December, she laughed and said, "I knowed I warn't wrong. I gits my check on the 17th. Yas, Lord, 'deed I does. I'se done got two of them five-dollar checks for the old age pension. It ain't but five dollars a month, but that sho' does help.

"Does you think all the old folkses will git it? I sho' hopes so, because old folkses what's done worked long as they can, needs it mighty bad now. There's a old man stayin' down this street what ain't got no folkses, and that pore old man is blind as a bat, and he don't git no pension. Not one Jesus thing does he git. Yas, Lord, is that right? Maybe they will git it fixed up for him so'se he can git a little help before they has to put him under the ground."

She resumed her rocking, and looking up, remarked, "When was the last time you seed Mr. Aaron?"

Without giving me time to reply, she continued, "I worked for his folkses till his mother and daddy moved away from here to go to New York. They was good folkses, if they was Jews. They was special good to us what worked for 'em. I just nearly about raised young Mr. Aaron.

"There was other boys in that family, but Mr. Aaron was my boy. Yassum, I 'spects he was bad as the rest of 'em, and I sho' had to give him a talkin' to sometimes, and I still talks to Mr. Aaron just like I wants to.

"He don't say nothin' back to me neither. He just laughs and says, 'Now, Gal, what's the matter with you?'

"But my Mr. Aaron ain't been to see me in a long time now, and just you tell him that Mariah said he'd better come, because she ain't got too old to git a holt of him yet, and she's 'spectin' him to send Santa Claus around to see her.

"See this scar on my neck? Well, that was one time I had to have a doctor. Let me tell you about it. A long time ago, when I was just as purt and hearty as I could be, a little bump come on my shoulder. For a long time, it warn't no size a-tall, then it started off to growin'.

"It growed till it hung plumb down over my shoulder. I warn't sick none, and it didn't hurt a-all, but I was scared it would keep on growin'.

"I went to see Miz Lora Fant. She's a colored woman that knows things. Atter she had done 'zamined that thing growin' on my shoulder, she run through her cyards and said, 'Miz Jackson, you'se been witched, but I'se glad I can tell you that you ain't been pizened. You was witched by a woman that lives right nigh where you stays. She has a grudge against you because it seems like to her you gits along so much better and has so much more than she does, so that's the grudge she is beholdin' against you.'

"Miss Lora said for me to come to town and git a certain kind of tobacco, and she explained just how I was to fix it up. She said she was going to do all she could for me, but I would be in bed and would have two more of them same kind of places to start growin' on me. She said that woman what had done witched me wouldn't come nigh me till the last of them places was gone. But then she would ask and inquire about me evvy day.

"Would you believe it? She done that very thing. She sho' did. When that place started on my neck, I got scared and went to see a man that knowed how to do things. I didn't tell him a word about me going to see Miss Lora, and that man told me word-for-word pre-zackly what Miss Lora had done told me, even about that woman. That he did!

"Then I knowed for sho' that I had done been witched. Then that old woman that had witched me started comin' to my neighbors evvy day to inquire about how Miz Jackson was, till they asked her why she didn't come see for herself how I was.

"I sho' was havin' me a time then, because one of them things commenced growin' under my arm, and I just had to lie in bed whilst they growed and growed. I sent for Miss Lora again, and she said they was ready to be lanced by a sho' enough doctor. I warn't real sure, so I sent for the old man I told you about a little while ago.

"He 'zamined me and said them places was ready to be lanced, and he allowed I would git well atter that, and then that woman would come evvy day to see how I was. When a doctor had cut open them places, that witch woman did start right out comin' to see me, but I didn't care, for she had done lost her power over me, and I got well.

"I'se got to see about them peas now," Mariah proclaimed in a tone that implied dismissal, so I began making ready for my departure.

"I wants to tell you something that'll make you always remember Old Mariah," she began, "It's what I'se heared all my born days, and I'se found that it's sho' the truth.

"Many things may tangle your foots, but tain't nothin' that can hold 'em. That's right. Ain't it?"

I thanked Mariah and promised to return but would not set a date for the next visit, as I did not want her to be disappointed.

She laughed. "That's because I said you and Mr. Aaron done lied to me about you comin'," she said. "Well, I still says you never come when you sent me word to expect you, and now you be sho' and tell Mr. Aaron I'se a-lookin' for him, too."

Mariah and her dog accompanied me to the door, and as I walked down the steps she said, "Chile, I'se sho' going to have lots of company atter you gits out of sight, but none of 'em ain't going to git nary a word out of Old Mariah about what your business with me was."

Three days later, as I passed the Southern Department Store, its proprietor, Mr. Aaron Stein [probably Abe Link], hailed me.

"What did you do to my good old nurse?" he demanded. "I let you go out to see her, and the next thing I hear, she has had a stroke and is at the point of death.

"I think it's mighty lucky that her story was recorded when it was, for it's not likely that she will ever be able to talk again."

The *Athens Banner-Herald* of December 21, 1938, carried the story of Mariah's death and announced that her funeral would be held from Ebenezer Baptist Church, Thursday, December 22nd, at two o'clock.

• • •

It was fortunate that I started out a little ahead of time to find the church, for I soon learned that there was more than one Ebenezer Church in, or near, Athens. Alexander and Freeman, undertakers in charge of the funeral, gave me directions for finding the place where the last respects would be paid to Mariah.

Finding that I still had a little time to spare before the funeral, I went by her "Mr. Aaron's" store to learn from him about her last few days. He said that her family had tried to prevent her from doing any hard work because they had known for several years that her blood pressure was very high. But while they were away at work, her restless energy and the industrious habits of her lifetime often led her to disobey their admonitions.

He said that she had waited for her children to go to work, and had "done a big washing," and this undue exertion was followed by a stroke of paralysis. She never spoke again, and died three days after she was stricken.

In conclusion he said, "She was a good woman, real smart, and just as honest as she could be. We will all miss her."

The funeral party had not arrived when I entered Ebenezer Church and took my seat near the rear of the auditorium. A woman, apparently a member of the choir, approached me at once and invited me to come up near the altar, where seats had been reserved for Mariah's white friends. There I could see and hear everything.

The altar was draped in white and banked with ferns. On it was an open Bible of immense size. Soon the message was carried to the organist that "they" were approaching. The people who had been standing in groups on the outsitde filed in and took their seats at the right and left of the room, but the entire center section had been reserved for the funeral party.

The sadly tender notes of the funeral music came from the piano as the doors were swung open and two preachers led the procession down the aisle. Not a word was spoken on the march to the altar. Immediately after the preachers were the six flower bearers, all of them elderly women, each carrying potted flowers and marching in couples.

Behind them, the casket on its wheeled stand was guided by an undertaker, and followed by the pallbearers. Then came Mariah's family, followed by their friends. Everyone in the church stood up until the funeral party was seated, and then the remaining seats in the center aisle were quickly filled by some of the others.

The choir sang "Nearer My God to Thee," and a preacher read as a text the Ninetieth Psalm, beginning with the words, "Lord, Thou has been our dwelling place in all generations," and in solemn and reverent tones he continued through its last verse, "And let the beauty of our Lord, our God be upon us: establish Thou the work of our hands upon us; yea, the work of our hands, establish Thou it."

The same preacher offered this prayer:

> Let us entreat Thee O, God!
> May we come before Thee,
> And ask Thee to console us,

And grant us Thy peace,
And help us.
We know Thou has never done wrong
But everything is for the good of Thy kingdom.
Bless these, Thy children,
And give them peace.
And when our time comes to go,
May we find a place in Heaven.

"We will now," he announced, "have the obituary of Sister Jackson, read by Miss Bessie Cannon."

A well-groomed, slender little woman left the section occupied by the family, and standing by the casket she began: "Sister Mariah Jackson was borned in the year of 1861, and was married to Brother Jackson at the age of twenty years. She was converted at the age of twenty-five, in Boggs Chapel, in Oglethorpe County, and when she came to Athens to live, she moved her membership to Ebenezer Church, where she has been well-known, and loved by all who knew her.

"Her husband died in 1930. She was the mother of fourteen children, eight of whom survive her. When sickness, death, or trouble came, she was always ready and willing to do all she could for the ones that needed her. Always cheerful and ready to help others, she was very industrious in her community until her death on December 20th, 1938."

The preacher invited the congregation to be comforted by a solo, "Fade, Fade, Each Earthly Joy," sung by Miss Mahala Wheeler. who arose and sang four stanzas of the old hymn.

Her voice, apparently almost strangled by emotion at times, indicated that her interpretative efforts stressed the meaning of the words rather than the tune and rhythm. Until this point the second preacher had not taken active part in the exercises. The presiding minister announced that Brother Stanley would now talk. His tribute ended with these words: "She lived like a child of God, and served Him long and well. Thou good and faithful servant, well done."

Brother Stanley then stated that he would turn the service back to Brother Roberts. This was the first time we had heard the name of the presiding cleric. He arose and began the funeral sermon, at the end of which the casket was opened.

The undertaker then invited me to be the first to view Mariah. The pianist had started playing a funeral march when I arose and went to the casket. While the dignity of death was on her face, as she lay there in her white robe in a casket of a delicate shade of lavender with white flowers, it seemed as though the old woman had just dropped off to sleep.

When I had returned to my place, the congregation filed by the casket in solemn procession, while one of the preachers droned in a low monotone, "The Lord hath given, the Lord hath taken away; blessed be the name of the Lord."

When all of the congregation had viewed her except the family, the undertaker lowered one side of the casket and rolled it close by each member of the family so they might see her, and even touch her, for the last time.

Now the chant of the preacher took on a newer and higher note and tone as he read the ritual of the church, while her children took their farewell.

"For as much as it hath pleased Almighty God, in His wise Providence to take out of the world the soul of the departed sister, " he read in ringing tones, and as the bier was wheeled back toward the altar he read the closing words: "From henceforth, blessed are the dead who die in the Lord, evenso saith the Spirit, for they rest from their labors."

The casket was closed. Brother Stanley uttered the benediction.

The flower bearers took their places, in couples, before the casket, and led by the two preachers, Mariah Jackson's body was followed by her family and friends as it was borne toward the cemetery. Just as she had prophesied less than a week before, she had answered the last call, and had gone, to return no more.

Life During Confederate Days

Editor's Note: The interview manuscript indicates this subject was Mrs. W. W. Mize, housekeeper, living at 198 Elbert St. The 1938 Athens City Directory lists her as Mary V. Mize, the widow of W. W. Mize, and she was living at the same address. No occupation is given. Mrs. Mize was interviewed Oct. 3, 1939, by Mrs. Ina B. Hawkes, and the manuscript was edited by Mrs. Maggie B. Freeman of the Athens WPA office.

Mrs. Mize was born in 1852. No records have been found concerning the date of her death.

• • •

Mrs. Mize's house completely fitted the description given to me by a delivery boy—located on a hill with a front yard practically covered in green grass with the exception of the front walk. There was shrubbery here and there, and a few blooming flowers about the yard. The tree leaves were beginning to show various colors, and presented quite a pretty picture.

The two-story frame house, painted white with green trimmings in the background, seemed a typical place to find just such a lovely old lady as I found occupying this home. In answer to my knock a lady appeared in a printed frock, rather spick-and-span, with quite a puzzled look on her face.

She probably took me for a book agent, since I carry my writing material, etc., and book agents are not given a very cordial welcome by most people.

"Good morning," she said, "won't you come in?"

Introducing myself, I asked, "Is there an older Mrs. Mize who lives here"

"Yes, come in," she said.

I accepted her invitation quite readily and as I entered the living room I saw an old lady with white hair and glasses, rocking to and fro and knitting something that seemed very interesting to her.

The heater was medium height, well-polished, displaying cleanliness itself. On this heater a kettle of water was boiling furiously. Over the mantle was a very old-style picture with a wide frame. In one corner was an old spinning wheel. A settee covered with worn silk tapestry and little silk balls dangling from it was in another corner. The antique chairs were showing their wear, and a large "art square" with a few rugs covered most of the floor.

"Howdy," said the elder Mrs. Mize, before I could tell her my name. The young Mrs. Mize following behind said, "Ma, this is Mrs. Hawkes; she wants to talk to you a while."

"Yes, yes, I am just knitting some lace for some pillow cases. I am always busy at something."

"Don't you want to tell me something about your life history, Mrs. Mize?" I asked.

At first she didn't know what to say, but then she said, "I can generally tell whether I like anyone or not the first time I see them, and I believe I will like you fine.

"Well, honey, my troubles and my joys might not be very interesting to you, but they have proven to be both interesting and sad to me.

"I was born eighty-seven years ago, June 22, 1852. My father was shot in the arm while in action during the Confederate War. He was sent home later because of illness and finally died with typhoid fever. He left Ma with six chilluns, three boys and three girls.

"I was the oldest and I had to help Ma raise the chilluns, but we worked hard. Everybody had to work hard then. I have seen people cry and beg for something to eat. But I took those chillun and sent them to school, and I made them help me when they got home.

"We did all kinds of field work. Mother and me had to make all our clothes, spin the cotton and weave the cloth. Child, we have had to sit at night, spin cotton and weave by a light'ood [fat-pine] knot for light a many a time.

"Our salt we got from the smoke house. We had folks to come to our smoke house many a time and get the dirt and boil it for salt. And we didn't have no sugar, either. Ma never let the syrup barrel get empty, unless she was cleaning it out to fill it again with fresh syrup.

"We sweetened pies, cakes and coffee with syrup and liked it as good as we like sugar today. Yes, sometimes now I make some old-fashion sweet bread, gingerbread, and I like it to this day.

"For coffee we parched wheat or rye. We didn't make enough wheat to have biscuits every day; we just baked biscuits twice a week. My mother would never let us cook on Sundays. We had to cook enough Saturdays to last till Monday.

"We was raised to go to church. I always saw that my brothers and sisters had good enough clothes to go. You see my oldest brother was a preacher—a fine Baptist preacher. My mother's father was a preacher; she had three brothers and one son that was preachers. I ain't bragging, but my people on both sides were good.

"Well, I began to think that I was grown about this time, and I married Mr. Mize, a fine young man, too. His father was the richest man in Franklin County. His land was five miles long and he owned two big stores. About the time we married, this land was in Franklin County. It was decided that Franklin County was too large, so it was divided, and the house that my husband was raised in is now the courthouse in Stephens County.

"I married in 1869, one night by candlelight. By then, times was a little better—we could afford candles. Carnesville was the nearest town to the Mize place.

"There was a lot of talk about the Mizes them days. Don't get me wrong, hear! I mean when they put the courthouse at the Mize's place. My mother was with us, and she wanted to go back to Tennessee. Mr. Mize said he came through Tennessee on his way back from the war, and he thought it was a beautiful country.

"I could not let Ma leave me, and we went back with her and stayed four years. I had two chilluns while I was out there.

"Mr. Mize was in the war. too, and he would sit and tell me lots of things that happened.

"He said one time him and one more of the men hid behind what they called the breastworks. He said it was something built of sticks and brush, just anything to keep the Yankees from seeing and killing them.

"One night it was raining and the trenches was full of mud. Him and this man got sticks and rails and put one end up on the fence. The other was down in the mud, but they rolled up in their blankets and stayed till daylight on these sticks, so they could see.

"Then they crawled out and saw a mother cat with three little kittens behind the breastworks. They had not had a bit to eat in three days, and they was so hungry that they got the little kittens, but they noticed that a mule had been shot, and they cut a plug out of him and cooked it and ate it.

"Oh, he said he had to do so many things like that, but he got back all right and we married.

"Well, honey, I kept on till I had fourteen chilluns, eleven boys and three girls.

"We went back to Franklin County and Mr. Mize's father died. So all his land and stores had to be divided up in eight parts. I took Mr. Mize's mother to live with us. We was not so well off and I had to work. Our wheat was not so plentiful either, but his mother had to have her biscuits three times a day. She had always been rich, you see, and she had to have anything she wanted.

"You see, when Mr. Mize's father died, his mother just got a child's part, but I didn't mistreat her. Mr. Mize thought sometimes that she was overbearing, but she was getting old, and we both looked over it the best we could. She lived with us and was ninety-seven years old when she died. My husband was her baby, too.

"Well, honey, as I told you we had fourteen healthy chilluns, and we were proud of every one of them. Some of them married before Mr. Mize died, in good families, too. Well, after Mr. Mize's death, I lived with my oldest son till he died. He was taken sick with pneumonia fever.

"Then I moved to Athens and have been here fifteen years. I got settled here and still sew, and do most anything that I can do, to help out as a boarder. I get thirty dollars a month from Mr. Mize's death.

"I had a daughter to die last year with appendix, but her husband has plenty, so he and the chilluns are very comfortable. My son had a bad wreck not long ago in his car and broke his neck. All this has caused me a lot of sorrow, but now I take my pension, and rent this house, because all we had has gotten out of our hands with all these hard times.

"My daughter, her husband and son, and his wife, and grandson and his wife stay here with me. I could not live if they didn't stay with me. You see they are here to take care of me, if I get sick, and look after everything. We have a cow, hog and chickens.

"My baby boy lives just a little ways up the road. He comes

every Saturday night or Sunday morning to hug my neck, and my grandchildren are so much company to me. There are five generations.

"I have forty grandchildren and fifty great-grandchildren. I am always getting some kind of little present because there is Mother's Day or Christmas and my birthdays, too. Last birthday I had 116 here. That's why I like roomy houses. We have right big rooms and two big porches to sit on."

Her daughter said, "Here Ma, here's your check."

Mrs. Mize's face brightened.

The young Mrs. Mize said, "Ma's always glad when her check comes. She wants to go to town right then and get it cashed."

"Do you go about much, Mrs. Mize?" I asked.

"Why, yes, I don't give up for little things such as a touch of rheumatism."

The noon train went by, so I decided I had better get to lunch. Mrs. Mize got up to go to the door with me and she said, "I am sorry we didn't know you was coming out. We would have had our house a little more in order."

"That's all right, everything looks very nice," I said.

It was just fairly furnished, but it was clean.

Fishermen

Editor's Note: This interview with J. H. Emerick of 157 First St., and his son, L. L. Emerick, was done Feb. 27, 1939, by Mrs. Grace McCune. The 1940 Athens City Directory lists a J. Henry Emerick as living at the same address. The 1920 federal census lists Joseph H. Emerick, of the First Street address as born about 1864 in Georgia. His wife's name was Anna.

In the 1938 city directory, his son, Lyman, is listed as being a painter and living at 150 Cemetery. Lyman is in the 1942 Athens City Directory as Lyman L. Emerick, married to Lillian E. Emerick. The 1920 census enumerates him as Lyman Emerick. J. H. Emerick is not listed in available Athens city directories after 1947. L. L. Emerick is not listed after the 1942 directory. The Social Security Death Index indicates a Lyman L. Emerick died in Bibb County, Georgia, aged seventy-one years, on Nov. 8, 1968. This dove-tails with 1920 census data, so it is probably the Athens Emerick. J. H. Emerick's house at 157 First Street was still standing and in good condition in 2001.

• • •

The rain was coming down in torrents as I started out in a taxi to get an interview with Mr. Emerick and his son about some of their fishing trips. As the taxi crossed the river and left the pavement, it turned around a curve and started up one of Georgia's famous old red [clay] hills.

It seemed to me that every time the car gained one foot, it slipped back two, and I was sure we would land in the river at the bottom of the hill. But the driver laughed, and said, "We'll make it, for I have already pulled this hill several times today."

The driver was right. We made it after several attempts, and I drew a breath of relief as he stopped in front of the house. Mr. Emerick and his son, Lee [Lyman], were in the back yard inside a long shed, looking over their fishing equipment.

I never knew it required so many things to be a fisherman. There were fish lines, and corks for pole fishing, as they called it, and trot lines and baskets that they used to keep their fish in after they were caught.

Then there were the steel traps used in trapping, and their camp stove. This was made, they explained, out of the steel rims of wagon wheels, as that was the best material they could get. The stove was a frame, made like a small table about eighteen inches high, with crosspieces across the top for the pans, pots and especially the coffee pot to sit on, so there was no danger of them turning over.

They assured me that with a good fire built under this stove, cooking was no problem. Picking up a large coffeepot, which would hold several gallons and was black from long use over many fires, Mr. Emerick said, "This old pot has been on many trips with me, and is just like an old friend. I would not know what to do without it. We always try to be comfortable when we go on our trips. I have a tent—also these," and he showed me several camp cots. "They go with us, also, and we have good blankets to keep us warm. We have dishes, too.

"Of course, they are tin cups and plates, for they can be carried around without any fear of breaking them.

"But why are you out in all this rain today? Just to ask me about fishing? Do you want to go fishing?

"No," I answered, "That is one thing I don't like to do. I can't be still long enough to fish and camp out. I went only one time," I replied, "and that was with my Dad and I didn't enjoy that.

"Why?" he asked. "I knew your Dad and he enjoyed a good fishing trip as much as anyone I ever knew, and I can't see why anyone could not enjoy it.

"Well," I admitted, "maybe you are not as afraid of snakes as I am." This brought a hearty laugh from both of them, and Lee said, "Just like a woman."

This was not my first visit to this home, as I had interviewed Mrs. Emerick a few weeks back for a life history of the mill village. She heard them laughing and came out to the shed where they were showing me their fishing things.

"What are they doing to you?" she asked. "Are they showing you those worms?"

Her son laughed again and said, "No, she would be afraid of them, for she is afraid of snakes—imagine that."

Mr. Emerick said, "Talking about women, just look at this new fish basket of mine—all the bottom cut out."

Mrs. Emerick laughed and said, "Yes I did it. He left the basket in the chicken yard, and one of my hens got in it to lay and she couldn't get out. I tried to get her out and couldn't, so I just cut the bottom out. Oh, yes, they both put up an argument, said the basket cost more than two or three old hens. But I didn't see it that way, and anyway, the hen is out and they can put in another wire bottom.

"Why don't you all come in the house to the fire?"

Laughing, she turned to me and said, "Tell him he is too old to be out in the rain."

I didn't say anything. I didn't know if I should or not, for the truth was he didn't look old to me. He and his son had on their overalls, and high-top boots. I saw only a tall, very erect man, apparently not over 50.

I was surprised when he laughed and said, "Don't mind Mammy, she is just reminding me that I was 75 yesterday."

I was sure they were teasing and I laughed. But he grinned and said: "It is a fact, yesterday was my birthday, and I am really that old, but I sure don't feel my age. But come on, we will go in the house. I want you to eat a piece of my cake. In fact, I had two cakes. My daughter brought me one, and of course Mammy cooked me one.

"But you know, neither one of them put any candles on them. I guess they just hated to remind me too much of my age. But I did have a nice day, for we was all at home together, and I got one of Mammy's hens for dinner. I liked to think it was the one that got into my new fish basket, but of course she wouldn't have killed that one for anything."

As we started into the house, I remembered my last visit here and the delicious dinner that I had with them. I regretted the sandwich I had before I left town. As we went through the clean, warm kitchen, I knew if they insisted I would never be able to resist dinner.

We went through the kitchen to a bedroom where a bright fire in the grate made the room comfortable. The son turned on the radio to get the news report, and for a few minutes they were quiet as they listened to the reports of a tornado in South Georgia.

"On the day before, that [South Georgia storm] was terrible," he said. "But I thought last week that we were going to be blown away. No," he said. "We wasn't here, but down on the river, away down in Greene County."

"How did you get down there?" I asked, "Surely you didn't go that far in a boat."

Mr. Emerick laughed and said, "You evidently don't know your old Oconee River. Why I have been as far as Milledgeville, Georgia, in my boat many times.

"But how do you manage about the dam," I asked, and I regretted that question immediately.

They both laughed and said, "Go over it." Then Mr. Emerick said, "We carry the boat in a truck and put it in the river below the dam, and after you pass the cemetery bridge, there is no more trouble. But speaking of the dam, have you ever been around it?"

"No," I replied, "I don't know why, but I just never have."

"Then, you should, and see those old pot holes, as they call them. Some of those holes are all of eighteen inches deep and dug out in solid rock. They are supposed to have been made by the Indians for cooking in.

"I have seen them ever since I was a small child, just large enough to follow my Daddy around. I guess that is where I get my love of fishing, for that was practically all he ever done was fish and hunt."

Mrs. Emerick came to the door, and said, "Come and eat dinner, then you can talk all the evening."

I thanked her and said I had already had my lunch before I left town

"But that was a long time ago, for you was here at eleven o'clock and now it is one p.m.," she insisted.

"When you get these men to talking, you will wish you had eaten, and besides, Grandpa wants you to eat some of his cake."

I admit it did not take very much insisting for me to accept. After dinner was over and we were back around the fire, I asked them to tell me about their trip to Greene County.

"Well," Mr. Emerick said, "We started out on the 11th day of January and didn't get back until the 17th of February. We did not intend to stay that long, but we got caught by the high waters and couldn't get away, for we was in our boat.

"I think it rained just about the hardest I have ever seen and the wind was terrible. I thought sometimes that our tent would

Still in good shape in 2001 was the home of J. H. Emerick
at 157 First St. in East Athens. *Photo credit:* Al Hester

go, in spite of all we could do, and if we had been up on the hill
it would have blown away, for trees were just torn up by the roots.
But we were down near the swamplands and the trees around us
protected us, I guess.

"Yet it is a wonder some of them didn't blow over on the tent.
No, we didn't have any luck on this trip. Usually we put out our
traps on creeks and rivers to catch minks and muskrats, but the
streams were so bad that we couldn't put out many traps, and in
all that time we only got about four minks and a few muskrats.

"We caught a few fish to eat, and caught a few squirrels and
some rabbits, but we had plenty to eat. The hardest thing was to
get enough dry wood for fires and cooking. But you know there
is always a way to get along if you try hard enough. Yet I don't like
to be out on trips much when the weather is so bad.

"Fishing is not what it has been, for I have seen the time when

I could make good money fishing and hunting. It was no trouble to sell all the fish we could catch, and get a good price for them.

"There was also a demand for game of all kinds, but the automobiles have changed all that, as well as they have changed many other things, even the railroads," he said.

"But just how have they affected fishing?" I asked.

"Well, almost everyone—or at least the greatest majority of people—own a car, and now it is no trouble for them to get out for a day of fishing or hunting. And in that way they get all the fish they want and game, too.

"You know it does not take you long in a car to go many miles and the roads are so much better. Why, I can remember when it would have been almost impossible to get near a river with a wagon. But now, you can ride to the banks of almost any river in a car. And just look at all the freight trucks as well as the passenger buses on the highways.

"No, there is no pay in fishing any more. We have to have a license to fish, another one if we sell them, and it means a different license in every county that you go in to hunt or fish. You can't sell game, either.

"There are so many people fishing now, that there are not as many fish as there were a few years ago. I really think Clarke County has less than any other county."

"What do you use for bait?" I asked.

"Well, that is according to how you fish, mostly. Just the common, old fish bait worm is good bait, and especially for pole fishing. Of course, some people like these baits that you buy. I mean these flies and things like that. I had rather hunt my own bait. There are many different kinds. One is the catawba worm or, 'catalpa' is the way it is spelled now, I think. But it used to be just plain catawba and you get them off a catawba tree.

"Did you ever see any catawba trees?"

"Yes, on a trip one time to North Carolina," I replied. "But I did not know there were many in Georgia.

"Why, I have some out here in my back yard," he said. "But you are right, there are more in North Carolina, and there is a river there, that I am told, is named Catawba, because of so many of these trees along the banks.

"But I put out my trees especially to get the worms for fishing. The common old grub worms make good fish bait. Ground puppies are also good but hard to get."

I didn't have any idea what "ground puppies" were and I was afraid to ask, as they had already laughed at me so many times. But I guess my expression showed my curiosity, for he said, "Did you ever see any 'ground puppies'?"

I hesitated, then very meekly admitted that I didn't know. They were having a grand time with me. But I had started out to learn something about how they fished, and I took it like a good sport and laughed with them.

"Didn't you ever go to school?" his son asked.

"Yes," I replied, "And I think I have owned a dog of most every kind, but I guess I just didn't ever own one of the 'ground puppies.'"

This brought a yell from them, and I knew I had said the wrong thing again. So I just grinned very sickly and asked what a "ground puppy" was.

After they got over their laugh, they explained that it was a worm. Mrs. Emerick also laughed with them, but said, "Don't let them get the best of you."

"I am trying not to," I replied, "but they seem to be doing it just the same. But if a 'ground puppy' is a worm, I want to know what kind of a worm it is."

Then Mr. Emerick said, "Well, it is really more like a lizard than a worm. It is found under old rotten logs on river banks, but the swamps are the best places for them. There are different kinds. The ones that we get around here are mostly a dark blue in color and just about three inches long.

"But down in Greene County, most of them are striped, dark blue and white, and are, I believe, just a little larger. There is just about two good bait in a 'dog.' They have a slime on them much like a snail.

"Then there is another kind that you find mostly in the dryer places that is a dark reddish color. I don't like to fool with them, as they are hard to find. I really don't know where they got the name of 'ground puppies,' but that is all I have ever heard them called.

"When we could fish with baskets—that is bait the basket and put it in the river—yes, the basket was tied to something on the bank to keep it from washing away, but it is against the law now to fish with a basket. The bait was old spoiled cheese. I have used many different baits: muskrat cooked is a very good bait, and raw meats, even the old grasshopper is fine bait for a hook, but it takes a mighty long time to get enough of these to try to fish with. A few years back when fish was plentiful, we really could catch fish in a basket.

"Did you ever see a trotline put out?" he asked.

I remembered little of the only fishing trip I ever made, and was afraid to say, but as he seemed to expect me to say something, I asked if it was a line that ran across the river for the small lines to fasten to, and for one time, I was at least partly right.

He said, "Well, you do at least know a little, don't you?" He grinned, and said, "But when we are fishing with trotlines, they are put out and baited at night and we do not go back to them until the next morning.

"How long have you fished?" I asked.

"Well, ever since I have been large enough to follow around

after my Daddy. He was a great fisherman. I have fished in all the streams in Clarke County, as well as other nearby counties. And I have really fished in this old Oconee River. I have had good luck, and bad luck in fishing.

"Many is the time I have went back to look at my hooks and found them all gone, but you will find some interesting things on the banks of the river. One of them is a very large Indian mound. It has been there so long that large trees are growing on it.

"I heard a few days ago that the government was going to open it and see what is in it."

"What kind of fish do you catch around here?" I asked.

"Well, they are mostly catfish, perch and minnows, but in the fresh water lakes you catch bass and perch. The largest fish I ever caught around here was a blue cat, weighing 21 pounds."

He laughed and said, "As long as you don't do any fishing, I will tell you this, fish are just like a woman. When they get excited and scared, why I have even had them to jump in the boat."

"Is that just a fish story?" I asked. "Or is it really facts?"

"I believe you are learning," he said. "I have really had that to happen; but I admit not often. But one time when I was on a fishing near Little Rock, Arkansas—and that is where I caught the largest fish I ever caught—and this is no fish story, either. It weighed a little over seventy-five pounds.

"Was I excited? Now, I really believe that you don't know any-thing about fishing, for anyone that has ever fished would know that the ambition of a fisherman is catch a large fish, and I don't know which was more excited, the fish, me or my little dog."

As he mentioned "dog," the yellow-and-brown dog lying at his feet raised her head to look at him. He reached down to pat its head and said, "No, it wasn't this one. It is dead, but now you can laugh, for it was just a little poodle dog.

"But she was a good sport, even if she was little, and would follow me, regardless of where I went. I have had to carry her lots of times because she was too small to keep up with me.

"But about the only time I ever saw her really scared was one day when we were fishing. She was asleep on my old coat in the bottom of the boat. I was trying to pull in a line, and evidently got the fish scared, for one jumped out of the water and fell on top of the dog, poor little thing.

"She gave a yelp, jumped and fell out of the boat." He laughed heartily, as he said: "You know, I thought I never would get her to come back to the boat, and she did hate to get wet so bad. After I got her back, I wrapped her up in the coat and we quit fishing for the day.

"And how I did enjoy seining. You use a net for that and just crowds of us would go seining and catch fish enough in just no time for a big fish fry, and that is really my greatest pleasure, a fishing trip off on a camp.

"I never did much fishing with a gill net, or as some call it a floating net. It is also against the law to use them any more, even in the open season for fishing.

"July and August are the best times for fishing around here. That is when I just can't stay off of a camp. I love the water and am happiest when I am on it. I only have two children. My son here and a daughter, but they are almost as bad about fishing as I am and have been with me many times.

"Lee will be just like me. In fact, he is now, and when he is not working on his job as a painter, you will find him off somewhere on the river fishing or hunting. My daughter is a good fisherman and can handle a boat like a man. That son of hers likes fishing.

"I used to take him with me, when he was very small."

"Do you make good with your trapping?" I asked.

"Sometimes, yes," he replied, "but even that is not so much now. Of course, if we could catch plenty of the game, it would pay fine.

"We stretch the skins out on a board and dry them out good before we strip them off. But you know we have plenty of fox here, and they are really getting bad, and something is going to have to be done about them or the country will soon be overrun with them.

"There are plenty of coons and 'possums here, too. Did you ever go hunting?" he asked.

"Well, one time," I replied, "but it was just a rabbit hunt, and I didn't catch anything."

He laughed and said, "Did you expect to catch them or kill them?"

"My brother killed several," I replied.

"I knew your brother," he said. "We used to go on many fishing trips together; he was a good sport, always ready to go his part in every way, work or play.

"My daddy was a member of the old volunteer fire company, and as I followed him in his love for fishing and hunting, I also belonged to the volunteer fire company. I was a member of the Bloomfield Hose and Reel Company No. 4. We were known as the 'Dirty Dozen.' There were several different companies and we had great times together, even if we were always trying to do just a little bit better than the other company.

"I still have a medal that was given my father by his old company, for his good service in 1873. I was one of the first ones that stayed on the fire department when it organized as a paid department in 1900.

"Back in those old days, there were two cisterns down on the main street and rain water was run into these cisterns from gutters to be used to fight fires. One of the companies had one of those old-time hand pumps and it took two men to use that pump to pump the water out of the cistern into another hose that would reach the fire.

"There was one or two companies of Negro volunteer firemen

then, also, and they really did some good work. I stayed on the
fire department about three years after it was reorganized and
then I gave it up and went on a fishing trip.

"I also worked at the waterworks plant here for years. Yes, I
have been on the police force. That was when we walked. There
was about nineteen men on the force, and two horses was all we
had to ride and they were used by the captain and chief.

"I remember when they bought the first automobile. We were
all supposed to learn how to run it, and do you know I haven't
learned until this day how to run an automobile and don't guess
I ever will. I could run it, start it all right, but when it came time
to turn around or back, I was out of luck. But then there was several of the boys that never learned how to run an automobile.

"But I just couldn't stay there long. I just had to get out—it is
just not in me to work where I can't go when I want to. I just can't
stay off the river long at a time, even if I am not making much
at it.

"But I have all this ground here and in season I raise vegetables
to sell. We have two cows, and I raise my own meat. We have
chickens. In fact it is almost like being out in the country and that
is what I like, for I had rather have contentment and peace than
riches any time.

"Every summer we go on a camp for weeks at a time, just
fishing—and how we do enjoy it. Oh, yes, we usually get a crowd.
Then we always have company over the weekend. They come out
on Saturday night after they get off from work, and if we are not
too far out they stay over until Monday morning.

"When we are camping too far away, they have to leave on
Sunday night. We always prepare for a large crowd on Saturday
night. That is when our fish baskets are nice, for we can keep fish
in them in the river for days at a time. And then when we are at
the camps, we have plenty of vegetables, chickens, eggs, butter

and milk, for it is no trouble to get all these things from the farmers that come to the camps. They make money by it, for all the camps that I have ever been around get tired of fish and want other things to eat."

His son came back into the room at this time and said, "You are going to have to spend the night."

"Why?" I asked.

"Because it is raining so hard you will not be able to get off this hill tonight," he explained.

"What time is it?" I asked, and was surprised to find it past five o'clock.

I began to think of how I was to get away. I said, "Well, I can get a taxi."

They laughed and said, "Do you want to bet on it?"

"But I don't see why I can't," I replied.

Mr. Emerick said, "Well, they don't like to come up this hill, for it is really bad, but still it is nothing to what it used to be."

I soon found that they were right, for I tried one hour and didn't get a taxi, and it was a long way to the bus line, but I decided to try to get to the bus. Anyway, I didn't much like the idea of riding down that hill. When I was ready to leave, I thanked them for their hospitality and that I had enjoyed the afternoon.

Mr. Emerick laughed and said, "We are very glad you came, for we have certainly enjoyed having you, and how about going fishing with us this summer? We will learn you how to fish, and all the different kind of baits and especially promise to show you what a 'ground puppy' is."

As I started down the steps. they all came to the porch with me, and Lee, their son said: "Wait just a few minutes. I think I see a car that belongs to one of my friends out at the store, and I will see if it is. I will ask him to take you to town."

"I don't like to be any trouble," I said.

"He won't mind," he said, and went on out to the store. He was back in a few minutes and said, "He will be glad to take you in to town, for that is where he is going, and he said he was ready to go whenever you was."

I said I was ready at any time, and as the man came out of the store, I said to them, "Good-bye."

As I was getting into the car, they reminded me of the fishing trip this summer. I thanked them, but I don't think I would like a fishing trip with them, for they would only have another grand time trying to "learn me how to fish."

Appendix I

Additional Information on the Rev. Alonzo C. Powers and His Family

The Alonzo Powers interview in this book in 1939 is one of the most interesting interviews because of the light it throws on the family of Harriet Powers, a former slave. She has become one of the most famous African-American folk artists through the creation of her "story" or "Bible" quilts in the nineteenth century. These quilts, using an African appliqué technique, tell Bible stories, folklore and also recount astronomical phenomena. One of these quilts is in the Smithsonian American History Museum and one in the Museum of Fine Arts in Boston.

The interview with the Rev. Alonzo C. Powers does not directly say that he was one of the children of Harriet and Armstead Powers, but as I checked the interview to verify several statements in it, it became apparent to me that it was quite likely that Alonzo was a son of Harriet and Armstead.

Harriet Powers was born a slave in Georgia on Oct. 29, 1837, according to Regenia A. Perry in her book, *Harriet Powers's Bible Quilts*. Armstead, her husband, also a slave, was born in September, 1832 in Georgia, according to the 1900 Clarke County federal census, which gave month and year of birth.

Alonzo reveals in his interview for the Federal Writers' Project that he was born a slave of slave parents in Madison County, Georgia, adjacent to Clarke County. He recounted some of his very early childhood memories of slavery, and it has been possible to verify portions of what he said. Through the interview with him, we know for the first time something of Harriet and Armstead Powers' early life in Madison County.

The Baptist minister sometimes indicated he was born about 1860, but his birth is listed in some censuses as being in 1865. The 1870 census indicates he was born about 1860, as does the 1880 census and the 1920 census. The 1865 date is given in the 1900 and 1910 censuses.

In the interview itself, Alonzo says he was born in 1859, but at the end of the interview he said he was ten years old at the time of the surrender in 1865.

Certainly if he were born in 1865, he would have no direct memories of slavery, although it would be likely he would remember what he had been told about the Civil War period.

The problem of recollections about slavery of blacks too young to have remembered it is discussed by George P. Rawick in his general introduction to *The American Slave: A Composite Autobiography* (Supplement, Series 1, v. 3 Georgia Narratives, Part 1).

He included some of these interviews, even though the persons interviewed were not born before 1865, ". . . because these narratives were for the most part not much different in tone and content from those of people who had in fact been slaves."

Rawick said:

> They indicate that the narratives were tapping an oral tradition about slavery among black people, as well as the "memories" of those who had been born as slaves. They provide a link between personal recollection on the one hand and "common knowledge," lore, and folksay, on the other, as historical source materials.

I believe that Alonzo Powers probably had early childhood memories of slavery, but if he did not, he faithfully passed on what was told to him. A reading of the Powers interview in 1939 shows vivid recollections and details, some of which can be checked.

Alonzo was married to Julia Jackson in 1881, in Clarke County, the marriage record listing him as "Lum" Powers. I talked with one mem-

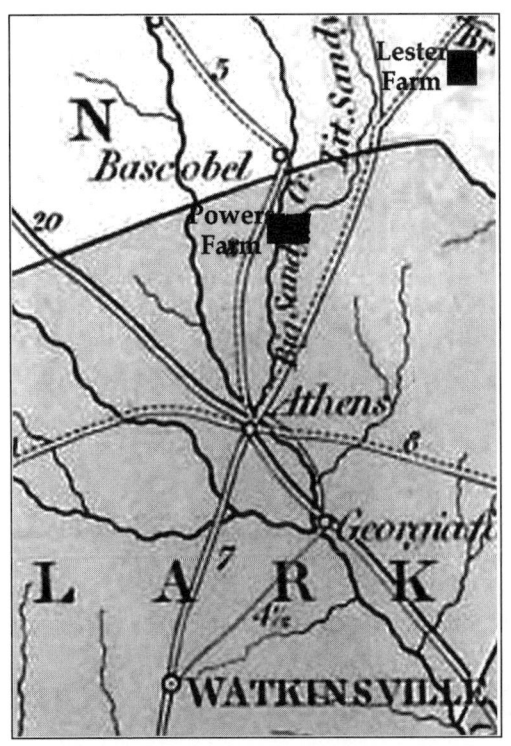

Map showing approximate location where Alonzo Powers was born a slave on the Lester farm in Madison County, and about where he and his parents lived after the Civil War in Clarke County near Sandy Creek.

ber of Thankful Baptist Church(a black church) in 2001 who remembered Alonzo and called him "Lum." The marriage date makes it more probable that he was born around 1860, marrying when about twenty-one years of age, although a marriage at sixteen would not be too unusual.

The birth date of about 1860 given in the 1870 census is especially persuasive, as he probably would not have given that date himself to the enumerator.

Alonzo indicates he was born in Madison County, six miles from Danielsville. This would put his birthplace about midway between Danielsville and Athens. He gives the names of Nancy and John Lester as the names of "my young Mistess and Marster."

There are numerous records showing that a Nancy and John Lester lived in Madison County on the same property. Nancy apparently was the widow of John Lester, Sr., one of the early settlers in Madison County. He is mentioned in the 1820 census for the county. He was involved in a court action appointing him guardian of his minor daughters in 1831 after they inherited an estate from Humphrey Hendrix.

These daughters were Caroline, Matilda, Harriet, Martha and Sally or Sarah. A Nancy Lester is listed as a family head, probably meaning she was a widow, in the 1840 Madison County federal census.

In 1871, Nancy in her old age deeded her 260-acre homeplace to her daughters Sarah H. Lester and Caroline Bullock, to repay them for caring for her. Her farm was about six-and-a-half to six-and-three-quarters miles north from Athens on the Danielsville Road, according to deed records.

Nancy was born in Virginia about 1785, according to the 1850 federal census for Madison County. She was listed as the 65-year-old family head, probably indicating that she was a widow. Living on the farm with her were John Lester, forty-one, apparently her son, and Sarah Lester, thirty-one, apparently her daughter. According to the census all the Lesters were illiterate.

The 1850 Madison County slave census indicated that Nancy had one forty-four-year-old male slave and one thirty-eight-year-old male slave; one forty-five-year-old female slave, one fifteen-year-old female slave and one twelve-year-old female slave. As we recall, Harriet Powers was born in October, 1837. At the time of enumeration in the slave census on Sept. 18, 1850, she would have been twelve years old, in keeping with the enumeration of a twelve-year-old female slave on the Lester farm. Alonzo also mentions that his grandmother was the cook for the Lesters. This woman could have been the female slave reported as 45 years old in the 1850 slave census, and it is likely she was the mother of Harriet. It is possible that Harriet Powers was named for Harriet Lester. Alonzo did not indicate in his interview how his father took the name of Powers, nor where the unusual given name of Armstead came from.

Curiously, there is another Armstead Powers listed in the Elmore County, Alabama, federal census of 1870. He is listed as being thirty-nine years of age. He had a family, and one of the children was named Amanda. No other names are the same. Alonzo also had a sister named Amanda. But Alonzo's father was enumerated in the 1870 Clarke County, Georgia, census with Harriet and their family, so the matter seems to be coincidental.

Nancy and the other Lesters are not listed as owners in the 1860 slave census, but this doesn't mean she had no slaves. Fairly frequently families were missed in various censuses. Nancy is enumerated as a 75-year-old farmer in the 1860 population census for Madison County. She had real property valued at $656 and personal property worth $4,320, according to the census. John Lester, 51, was also listed as a farmer, living in the same dwelling with Nancy. Sarah was still at home, but had cut a bit from her age, being enumerated as age thirty-eight. Living in an adjacent dwelling was Caroline Bullock, forty-nine years old, listed as family head and "farmer." With her was Mary Ann Bullock, twenty-four; and Harriet Bullock, twenty-two years of age. Caroline was illiterate, and we assume she was a widow.

Alonzo speaks of a "young master" whom we cannot identify in the various censuses of the county. We do know, however, that Caroline Lester had a brother, John H. Lester. On Dec. 22, 1862, he wrote a will leaving his gold watch to his "beloved sister."

The will was recorded June 10, 1863. He supposedly died in the war. Alonzo says in the interview that his young master was killed in the war.

A John H. Lester was a private for the Confederacy and was killed in 1863 defending Vicksburg, Mississippi. He, however, belonged to Company "K" of the 40th Regiment of Georgia Volunteer Infantry, called the "Haralson Invincibles" from Haralson County, Georgia. Haralson County is far west of Madison County, being nearly in Alabama.

It is not likely that an Alonzo born about 1860 would remember his "young marster" giving him an apple as he headed off to war, as he remembers in the interview in 1939, but he may have been told this occurred. Or if he really were ten years old at the war's end, as he says at the end of the 1939 interview, he certainly could have remembered it.

I have been unable to confirm that John Lester had an older brother, Franklin, who Alonzo indicates was tortured by the Yankees. Alonzo mentions that his "young marster" served in place of Franklin in the Civil War.

The Lester family was not especially well off, nor did it own large amounts of land and slaves. While a pioneer family, Lesters did not hold major public offices or serve as heads of grand juries in Madison County, records show. There is no record in existing cemetery indices for Madison County indicating where John Lester, Sr., John Lester, Jr., John H. Lester or Nancy Lester are buried.

Alonzo also reveals in his 1939 interview that his father, Armstead, was a slave owned by Jimmie Nunn, or "Mr. Jimmie," who lived on the Danielsville Road. There was indeed a James Nunn living on property he had purchased on Sandy Creek in Madison County, not very far from the Lester farm. He may have also owned other property. Alonzo says his father was able to visit his mother twice weekly.

James Nunn was enumerated as a fifty-nine-year-old, literate overseer in the 1860 Madison County census. His real property was worth $1,200 and his personal worth was $1,900. In the 1860 slave census, he was shown as owning one slave, a 22-year-old male. This does not agree with Armstead's birth year of 1832, shown in the federal censuses.

James had purchased his land from Benjamin Brown for two hundred dollars in 1856, according to the deed in the Madison County court house.

On July 22, 1861 James Nunn took an oath he would not sell liquor to slaves without permission, or to free persons of color without approval of their guardians. He paid five dollars to sell spirituous liquors from his home and posted a $500 bond to assure keeping it orderly, according to county records.

Alonzo Powers seems to get high marks for the general accuracy of his account of slave days, on points we can check. The evidence is very strong that he and his mother, Harriet, lived on the Lester farm during the Civil War. His father, Armstead, may have been the only slave of James Nunn, who lived not far away. Alonzo's account of "young marster" going off to fight in the Civil War may well be true, but more research is needed.

Alonzo's account probably is generally accurate, although he may have passed on the stories of his parents, as well as his own memories. The interview does shed new light on the background of Harriet Powers and shows that she lived in Madison County and was probably born there. It also indicates that she was a slave, along with her mother, belonging to Nancy and John Lester.

As Alonzo says, the post-war period brought a change of residence to the Powers family, although they moved only a few miles away to northern Clarke County.

The 1870 Clarke County federal census confirms Alonzo's statement the Powers family moved after the war from Madison County and settled north of Athens in Sandy Creek Militia District, #219. Armstead is listed as a farm laborer and Harriet is shown as "keeping house." Neither could read nor write, and they owned no real estate. They did, however, have a personal worth of $300, according to the census.

Living with them were some of their children, Amanda, fifteen; Leonzoe [sic], ten; and Nancy, four. "Leonzoe" is obviously Alonzo. The 1880 census of Clarke County found the Powers family still living in the Sandy Creek Militia District, although they are enumerated as the Armstead "Powell" household. The family members are listed as Armstead, 38; Harriet, 34, his wife; Alonzo C., 19, a son; a daughter, Lizzie, 12; and another son, Marshall, 7. The enumerator indicated Harriet was literate, as was Alonzo. The 1900 census, however, shows Harriet not able to read and write. There is no 1890 federal census for

Clarke County, as most of that federal census was destroyed in a fire in Washington, D. C.

It was the enumeration of the Powers family in the 1870 and 1880 censuses that gave conclusive evidence Alonzo C. Powers was the son of Harriet and Armstead. I had read earlier that he was their eldest son in Regenia A. Perry's book, *Harriet Powers's Bible Quilts.* She wrote that Harriet had probably been a member of New Grove Baptist Church in the Sandy Creek area and that her eldest son, Alonzo, was the church's first clerk. She did not, however, give any source for this information.

I was doing research to determine what property the Powers family owned in Clarke County when as a "long shot" I looked up the deed for the New Grove church. I thought perhaps Alonzo would be mentioned as a party to the deed establishing the church.

Current church members and their minister, Dr. James Washington, had no information in 2001 linking Harriet and Alonzo together. They had not heard of Alonzo, nor had they seen the deed for the property for the first New Grove church.

An "Alonza [*sic*] Powers colored" was indeed listed as one of the New Grove trustees to which John Winter, a white landowner, on July 11, 1883, deeded about 1.5 acres ". . . in consideration for the love and affection he has for the Christian religion."

I haven't found any marriage records concerning Harriet and Armstead. Slaves could not legally be married, although many had ceremonies performed, varying from those with a minister to less formal "jumping the broom" ceremonies mentioned by Alonzo in his interview. They considered themselves to be "married," about 1856, based upon data in the 1900 census for Clarke County, which indicates they had been married for forty-four years. Harriet was the mother of nine children, but only three were living in 1900, according to the census.

Apparently the Powers family was typical of many black families after the Civil War, for as census records show, they rented their land. As the century waned, however, this would change. In the last decade or so of the century, they managed to purchase very small amounts of farmland in the Sandy Creek area, according to Clarke County deed records. A description of one tract in its later sale by them indicates it was located on the "Old Clarkesville Road" near McGinty's Store. No deed of purchase has been found for them of this property.

It is not clear today which road the "old Clarkesville Road" was. Several different roads can be taken to Clarkesville, northeast of Athens. A mortgage taken out with their land as part of the collateral indicates the Powers family lived adjacent to the "Kendrick" property. An old map shows that the Kendricks lived on Harmony Grove Road, an old road to Harmony Grove (present-day Commerce), and from there north to Clarkesville.

Regenia Perry in her book says that the Powers couple bought their land in the 1880s, although I haven't been able to document this. In the 1870 census, they own no real property. Property ownership, however, is confirmed by the 1900 census, which lists Armstead as owning his farm, although it was mortgaged.

Regenia Perry writes that the land was mortgaged to buy a buggy, but I haven't found this information.

Armstead is shown as conveying, on March 30, 1891, about two acres of land in the Sandy Creek area to J. R. Crawford, thus indicating he owned the property prior to that time. Harriet is not a party to the transaction. Crawford had loaned $177.80 to Armstead with the land as part of the security.

It would appear that Armstead was forced to sell this property to make good on a mortgage note to Crawford, which came due after Oct. 15, 1891. He also used as security "one gray mule, about 12 years old, known as Escue mule, and one Clay Back Texas pony, known as the Addington Pony." A man named Addington witnessed the legal papers on the mortgage.

Curiously, a parcel with the exact description was also sold by Armstead and Harriet to J. R. Crawford, but this time for $359.17. Harriet is not listed as owning the land with Armstead in the first transaction, but she is listed with him in the second sale on March 5, 1901. It may be that the description given was for the entire parcel, and a lazy clerk didn't bother to give the boundaries of each sale properly.

The family's poor economic condition also forced Armstead to mortgage one 400-pound bale of cotton "now being grown on my place on Sandy Creek Bridge Rd., adjoining lands of Thornton Kendrick." Sandy Creek Bridge Road may have been another name used for the Harmony Grove Road, or could have been a nearby road. J. N. Booth loaned Armstead $12.50 on July 17, 1892, with the cotton as security.

Alonzo, too, was having a hard time. On March 21, 1892, he received twenty dollars for mortgaging his "sorrell 12-year-old horse Bill" to McAlpin & Pittard, according to Clarke County mortgage book records.

Armstead and Harriet apparently sold additional land in other transactions. I have found a sale by Harriet Powers to C. W. Cooper on Aug. 30, 1897, and by Harriet A. Powers, et al., to J. R. Crawford on March 5, 1901, as already mentioned.

The Clarke County "colored" and white yearly tax digests are fragmented and incomplete in the nineteenth century, but do throw more light on the Powers family. Armstead Powers is shown as having paid his poll tax in 1884 in the Buck Branch Militia District #225. Buck Branch adjoins the Sandy Creek Militia District. In order to vote, all males twenty-one years of age or over had to pay their poll tax, which varied in amount from fifty cents to one dollar yearly.

Armstead also had horses and cattle valued at ninety dollars, a fifty-dollar valuation of household and kitchen furniture and five dollars worth of plantation and mechanical tools. He had other property valued at thirty dollars and paid a total tax of $1.70 for the year. He was not assessed anything on land.

Alonzo Powers in 1884 is listed on the next line below Armstead as being assessed taxes in the Buck Branch District. He paid his poll tax and had five dollars worth of household and kitchen furniture. He paid a one dollar poll tax and two cents as additional property tax.

In an undated fragmentary tax digest for the Buck Branch Militia District, Alonzo is again shown paying his one dollar poll tax and one-and-a-half cent tax bill. In the same fragmentary digest for the Sandy Creek Militia District, Armstead Powers is assessed his poll tax, and a valuation of twenty-five dollars is placed on household and kitchen furnture, and five dollars for plantation and mechanical tools.

In the 1892 tax digest, Armstead was living in Sandy Creek Militia District and is for the first time we know of assessed on land holdings— three acres valued at $135. He had horses and cattle valued at seventy dollars and $105 valuation of household and kitchen furnishings, with plantation and mechanical tools valued at twenty-five dollars. He had other property valued at ten dollars.

Also in 1892, Alonzo paid his poll tax and had horses and mules valued at forty dollars and ten dollars value for kitchen and household furniture, but wasn't taxed on any land.

The 1894 tax digest gives us our first insight into Harriet's ownership of land. She is taxed on three acres of land in the Sandy Creek Militia District, valued at $150. She had horses, mules and other stock worth sixty-five dollars. She had seventy-five dollars value in household goods, thirty-five dollars in plantation and mechanical tools and a ten-dollar valuation of other property

An "Arms" Powers in the 1894 digest is also taxed for three acres of land, valued at 150 dollars. He has household goods worth ninety-five dollars, fifty dollars valuation for horses and mules and thirty dollars in plantation and mechanical tools, with ten dollars value for other property.

It would appear that the husband and wife owned land and other taxable items separately and possibly at different locations. Regenia Perry states that the couple separated about 1895, but gives no source for this. As early as 1889, however, Armstead was listed in the city directory as living in Athens, but Harriet is not listed. This might imply separate residences.

Also in 1894, their son, Marshall, paid a poll tax and was taxed on one acre of land in the Sandy Creek Militia District. Alonzo, in Buck Branch Militia District, paid his poll tax and had twenty dollars worth of houshold and kitchen furniture.

The 1896 tax digest shows Harriet taxed on four acres of land valued at 200 dollars, plus forty-five dollars worth of household and kitchen furniture; and twenty-five dollars in tools. Her son, Marshall, paid his poll tax, but paid no other tax.

Alonzo Powers in Buck Branch Militia District paid his poll tax and was taxed on twenty dollars worth of horses, etc.; and ten dollars in household furnishings.

No further tax records have been checked for later years, at this writing.

We do know that Alonzo acquired a bit of country property himself. In a Clarke County deed, Alonzo is shown receiving three acres of land "by virtue of a bond of title" from Benjamin B. Williams. On Nov. 13, 1919, the administrix of Williams' estate, Mrs. F.O. Williams, sold the land to Alonzo for $300. Thus, Alonzo had to pay for land which had already seemed to be his.

This land was on the old Athens-Elberton Road in the Buck Branch Militia District. It was the land that had in 1853 been given to the Moore's Grove Church by Richard D. Moore for use as a church site. Apparently Alonzo lived there after the church ceased to function, and the land reverted to Richard Moore, who sold it to Benjamin Williams.

Alonzo is listed in the 1900 Clarke County census as living in the Buck Branch Militia District, with his occupation given as "minister," thus confirming his statement in the interview that he was a preacher. The same census indicates that he was renting his place of residence at that time.

On Nov. 6, 1919, Alonzo had given a warranty deed on the land to the Bank of Statham to secure a debt. The debt was paid in 1921 and Alonzo apparently had the land free and clear at Moore's Grove. That same year he sold the land to A.M. McCluskey for $444.28, according to deed records.

Alonzo indicates in the interview that he preached in many different communities in Clarke and other nearby counties. I haven't yet found any record of him in Clarke County between 1921 and 1938, when he is shown in the city directory as renting a house in Bray's Alley, just off the Danielsville Road, on the north side of Athens.

The 1900 federal census for Clarke County lists Harriet and Armstead as husband and wife, living on the Sandy Creek farm, but there are other indications they were going their separate ways. As mentioned, Armstead is listed in the 1889 Athens City Directory as a laborer living at 27 Angle St., running off Arch Street in East Athens. Harriet is not listed with him.

Alonzo Powers apparently continued to live in the Buck Branch area north of Athens, as we find no mention of him in early Athens directories. His brother, Marshall, however, is listed in the 1904 directory as being a bricklayer living in Barberville, which was on the north side of Athens. He would continue to live there at least until about 1920, according to city directories.

It was in 1886 that Harriet Powers exhibited her "Bible" quilt at a fair in Clarke County, according to Reginia Perry. A local art teacher admired it, but could not persuade Harriet to sell the quilt until about 1891, and then only because of Harriet's and Armstead's poverty. Her second quilt was to become famous after it was exhibited in Nashville in 1898, according to Regenia Perry. Mary E. Lyons, however, says in her book *Stitching Stars: The Story Quilts of Harriet Powers,* that the quilt was exhibited at the Atlanta Cotton States Exposition in 1895.

Harriet seems to have become quite poor and may have lived in the Buck Branch area according to Regenia Perry. Harriet died in 1911, Perry wrote, with a personal worth of only seventy dollars. Armstead apparently worked in Athens as a laborer and died before Harriet after their relationship ended.

According to Alonzo's interview, his family scattered. We know that he was listed in the 1938 and 1940 Athens city directories, but he is not in the 1942 directory. It is possible he may have moved out-of-state with one of his children, or he may have died about that time. My attempts to locate Powers family members who might know more about Alonzo have failed. As of 2001 I don't know when and where Alonzo died or where he is buried. There is no record of his death in the Georgia Death Index, the Social Security Death Index or any of the Clarke County cemetery listings.

Appendix II

Instructions to Writers Preparing WPA Life Histories

Editor's Note: These instructions were made available to writers involved in the interviewing and writing process for the Federal Writers' Project throughout the South.

1. Materials are to be collected on tenant farmers and their families, farm owners and their families, cotton mill villagers and their families, persons and their families in service occupations in towns and cities, and persons and their families in miscellaneous occupations such as lumbering, mining, fishing, turpentining. Samples showing the nature of the materials to be collected are attached hereto.

2. The life histories may range from approximately two thousand words to ten or fifteen thousand words, depending upon the interest of the material.

3. An outline is attached hereto. This outline shows the nature of the subject matter which should be covered in the life history. However, it is not desired that each life history or story follow this outline in a rigid manner. The stories will not be useable if they are constructed on a rigid pattern. For instance, the writer may reverse the order of the outline, he may begin with any item which he considers of special importance in the case under consideration, he may follow the whole outline or limit himself to a part of it in any particular story. It is immaterial whether the stories are written in the first, second, or third person. Insofar as possible, the stories should be told in the words of the persons who are consulted. The effort should be made to get defi-

nite information. Avoid generalities such as "those who are industrious and ambitious can do well," "had not made good use of opportunities"—wherever possible expand such wording to give detail, that is, exactly what industry and ambition might have done or what the opportunities were that could have been used. In general avoid the expression of judgment. The writer will, of course, have to exercise judgment in determining the course of a conversation through which he gains information, but aside from this, he should keep his own opinions and feelings in the background as much as possible. For instance, if he sees people living under conditions which he thinks are terrible, he should be most careful not to express his opinion in any way and thus possibly affect the real feeling of the person consulted and must record this feeling regardless of his own attitude toward it. Any story in which this principle is violated will be worthless.

4. Writers should not limit themselves to the types of stories shown in the samples. It is hoped that original modes of presenting the material will be developed. The criteria to be observed are those of accuracy, human interest, social importance, literary excellence. It may not be possible to combine all these in any one story. However, accuracy and literary excellence should be present in all. A story of some very exceptional family may be of great human interest but of minor social importance. The best stories will be those which combine all these elements. (By accuracy, it was explained in conferences, is meant simply write what you smell, see, hear. Writers cannot check on the accuracy of what is said. Get in the subject's own words what he has done, felt, and thought. If the subject's head is filled with wrong notions, foolish thoughts, and misinformation, if this kind of materials comes out in conversation, record it. Let the subject's mind speak for itself.)

5. While the majority of stories should be about families and should attempt to include information on all the points listed in the attached outline, it may be best in some instances to write about a section of a village or a community dealing with all the families in that section or community; or a story may be written about any one of the items in the outline, such as, for instance, the size of the family, the coming of chil-

dren and the effect their coming has on the fortunes of the family. Any town, community, village or open country from which a number of stories are secured should itself be described in a separate story.

6. Some topics of importance may come up which are not covered in the outline. It will be best to go ahead and treat such topics and not wait to ask for permission to deal with them. However, no state director should allow writers to abandon the outline and sample stories to such an extent as to change the nature of the work.

7. All the stories do not have to be solemn and packed with information. If an amusing incident reveals the attitude of a family towards some important problem then this incident should be related.

8. The purpose of this work is to secure material which will give an accurate, honest, interesting, and fairly comprehensive view of the kind of life that is lived by the majority of the people in the South. It is extremely important that families be fairly selected, that those which get along well or fairly well be selected for stories as well as those that make a less favorable impression. The sub-normal, the normal, the above normal, all should have stories written about them As the work gets along, it will be necessary to expand it in order to include other important groups, but insofar as possible, a beginning should be made with the groups indicated above. In those parts of the South where cotton textile manufacturing is unimportant, and other industires dominate the scene, these other industries should be selected for treatment. For instance, in and around Birmingham, Alabama, both families in textile manufacturing and families working in coal and iron industries should be treated.

9. Each story should carry on the first page the date when the first version was written, the name of the writer and the name and address of the family written about. This information needs to be given for purposes of verification. Names will be changed in any material that is published.

10. It is hoped that out of this material four or five volumes will be secured which can be published under a series name such as LIFE IN THE SOUTH with individual names for each volume.

Appendix III
List of Athens Life Histories

NAME OF INTERVIEWEE	TITLE	OCCUPATION
Bradley, Louie D., Mrs.	Reminiscence	WPA worker
Bramblett, Lelia, Mrs.	Princeton Factory Memories	not listed
Crane, George Shaw	Edward Wolcott	landlord
Crawford, Luther, Mrs.	God Helped Us	farmer
Crowder, Grace, Mrs.	Patent Medicine Vender	tailor
Davis, Margaret, Mrs.	Life History	not listed
Dudley, J. Buford	Bargain House	merchant
Emerick, J. H.	Fisherman	fisherman
Gordon, Texie, Mrs.	The Boarding House	owner
Hardee, Charles S. H.	College Memories	not listed
Harris, Janie Bradberry Mrs.	Janie Bradberry Harris	not listed
Hill, Mary Wright (Negro)	Principal of Grammar Sch	principal
Hill, Sarah (Negro)	Bea, the Wash. Woman	laundress
Jackson, Lucille (Negro)	De Troubles I'se Seen	laundress
Jackson, Mariah (Negro)	Cindy Wright	midwife
Johnson, Andrew (Negro)	A Good Investment	insurance agent
Johnson, Lisa (Negro)	I'se a Fast 'Oman	midwife
Johnson, Mary (Negro)	Neg. Life on a Farm	farmer
Jones, Willie	A Visit to a Flower Shop	florist
Jones, Willie	House of Flowers	florist
Lewis, James, Mr. & Mrs.	Making the Best of It	merchants
McLeroy, James L.	The Successful Farmer	farmer
Michael, Moina Belle	The Poppy Lady (frags)	not listed
Mize, W. W., Mrs.	Life During Confederate Days	housekeeper
Moon, Mrs. H. G.	The Unwelcome Caller	bill collector
Power(s), Alonzo (Negro)	Reminiscence of a N. Preacher	preacher
Seagraves, Edna	Where Beauty Is Assured	beauty operators
Shorrow (?), Kent (Negro)	My Ups and Downs	farmer
Southern Dept. Store	A Day in a Store	Southern Dept Store
Waller, Nick (Negro)	Preacher-life history	preacher, farmer
Webb, Joseph Eliot	Mr. Doolittle—Lawyer	attorney
White, Omie Williams Epps	An Air-Minded Family	saleslady
White, Sue S., Mrs	Mildred Lawson Beauty Shop	beautician
Whitehead, L.S., Mr. & Mrs.	New Way Cleaning	dry cleaning firm
Willingham, Mary (Negro)	I Ain't No Midwife	practical nurse
Wood, Josephine, Mrs.	A Visit with Aunt Joe	not listed

Index

A Word about the Editor

Al Hester has lived in Athens for twenty-nine years, and is constantly amazed at the history and culture of the town. He retired in 1997 as Director of the James M. Cox, Jr., Center for International Mass Communication Training and Research at the University of Georgia. The Center, working with a grant from the James M. Cox, Jr., Foundation, gave training and education opportunities to several thousand journalists and students, mainly from developing countries or former communist countries.

Over the course of his directorship, he led training, education and research workshops and seminars attended by persons from more than three dozen nations.

Receiving his Ph.D. in mass communication from the University of Wisconsin, Madison, he came to teach at the Henry W. Grady College of Journalism and Mass Communication. He was department head of the News-Editorial Department for eight years and also taught reporting, editing, magazine writing and international communications.

A native Texan, Dr. Hester was education reporter, local government reporter, assistant city editor and city editor of *The Dallas Times Herald* in Dallas, Texas. He received his bachelor's and master's degrees at Southern Methodist University in Dallas.

The author or editor of nearly a dozen books, Dr. Hester has also been an active magazine free-lancer and has written and sold more than 200 non-fiction articles.

He is the co-author with his wife Conoly of *Athens, Georgia: Celebrating 200 Years at the Millenium.* Since his retirement he has founded The Green Berry Press, which has just published a new edition of

Michael Thurmond's *A Story Untold: Black Men and Women in Athens History.*

Dr. Hester is a member of the Athens-Clarke Heritage Foundation, the Five Points Association, and Vernacular Georgia, a statewide organization devoted to the study and preservation of everyday buildings and dwellings.

He and Conoly have two children, Katherine L. Hester of Atlanta and Al C. Hester of Columbia, S.C.